New NF INF

745.59
S11c

SEP 1 2008

S0-AFG-610

CREATING
Candles

WITHDRAWN
MENASHA'S PUBLIC LIBRARY

0 11557 03476 9

Copyright © 2008 by Stackpole Books
Copyright © 2003 by RCS Collezionabili S.p.A., Milano
Copyright © 2001 by RCS Libri S.p.A., Milano
Originally published in 2001 by RCS Libri S.p.A., Milano

Published by
STACKPOLE BOOKS
5067 Ritter Road
Mechanicsburg, PA 17055
www.stackpolebooks.com

All rights reserved, including the right to reproduce this book or portions thereof
in any form or by any means, electronic or mechanical, including photocopying,
recording, or by any information storage and retrieval system, without
permission in writing from the publisher. All inquiries should be addressed to
Stackpole Books, 5067 Ritter Road, Mechanicsburg, PA 17055.

Printed in China

10 9 8 7 6 5 4 3 2 1

First edition

Directing Editor: Luisa Sacchi
Coordinating Editor: Annamaria Palo
Cover design by Giusi Mauri

Library of Congress Cataloging-in-Publication Data

Sacchi, Luisa.
   Creating candles / Luisa Sacchi. — 1st.ed.
      p. cm.
   ISBN-13: 978-0-8117-3476-9
   ISBN-10: 0-8117-3476-5
   1. Candlemaking. I. Title.

TT896.5.S32 2008
745.593'32—dc22

2007040772

CREATING
Candles

Luisa Sacchi

ELISHA D. SMITH PUBLIC LIBRARY
MENASHA, WISCONSIN

STACKPOLE
BOOKS

Contents

Techniques

MATERIALS

The materials and equipment used to make candles are inexpensive and easy to find; most items are available at craft centers or from online retailers.

What You'll Need

1 Paraffin wax
Paraffin wax is sold by weight in craft centers. It comes in the form of flakes or small granules and is the core ingredient in creating candles.

2 Stearin
This white powder, another necessary candle-making ingredient, is mixed with wax to give the candle a more luminous appearance; it also allows the candle to burn better. The standard ratio is 1:10—1 spoonful of stearin to 10 spoonfuls of wax.

3 Gel wax
Gel wax is an increasingly popular candle-making product. It looks like clear gelatin; after melting the gel in a double boiler or microwave, you can add a variety of objects to it, which will remain visible in the finished candle.

4 Old candles
An alternative to melting wax flakes, granules, or gel is to simply melt down old candles. This is an inexpensive option because the wax is often already colored and scented. The final product, however, may provide less light than one created with raw materials.

5 Small pots
You can use two small pots or a double boiler to melt the candle wax (with two pots, the larger one should hold about 3 inches of water; the smaller one will be used to melt the wax).
It's important that the wax never come into direct contact with the heat source because it could catch on fire.

6 Coloring
You can color the wax using the following materials:
- Colored disks, found in most craft centers
- Wax crayons, although the disadvantage of this material is that it makes the wax more opaque
- Liquid colors (mainly for gel wax)— use only a few drops, especially if you want to maintain the gel's transparency.

7 Scents
Candle-scenting oils are available in almost every imaginable scent. You need to use only a few drops to create an intense aroma. Never use scents that contain alcohol as they are highly flammable.

8 Modeling clay
Use modeling clay to secure the area where the wick passes through the wax to ensure it doesn't slip back into the wax. Clay is not necessary when making a candle in a container.

9 Wicks
Wicks come unwaxed in long strands or already waxed and fitted with a metal base; to make container candles, you'll usually have to snip off the base.

10 Needles
A candle-making needle is used to pierce the semihardened surface of the wax in order to insert the wick.

11 Wooden skewers
To ensure the wick remains vertical when inserted into still-warm wax, wrap the tip of it around a wooden skewer and lay the stick across the top rim of the container.

12 Thermometer
This is a useful tool, especially if your melting equipment doesn't have its own temperature gauge. Wax is very temperature sensitive and can reach a flash point very quickly. Depending on the wax, this temperature can be as low as 290°F.

This simple candle project, made in a container of glass, ceramic, terra-cotta, or wood, will illustrate basic candle-making techniques.

Melt the wax

Pour 10 spoonfuls of wax and 1 spoonful of stearin in a small pot, then place the small pot in a larger pot filled with about 3 inches of water. Place them both on the stove and melt the mixture over a low setting.

Color the wax

Once it's melted, you can color the wax using coloring disks, liquids, or crayons. Add the color, then gently stir the mixture with a spoon to ensure the color is evenly dispersed.

Scent the wax

Add about 8 drops of scenting oil to the wax—more for a stronger scent, less for a weaker scent. Stir to mix the oil thoroughly.

Cool the wax

Slowly pour the compound into the candle container. Let it air dry for approximately 1 hour. *Do not put the wax into a refrigerator*—if it cools too quickly, the wax will sink in the center. Remember to insert the wick (next step) before the wax cools completely.

Insert the wick

If the wick has an attached base, snip it off. While the wax is still soft, pierce through its center with a needle and insert the waxed wick. Trim to the desired height.

TIPS AND TRICKS

- To avoid a mess, protect your work area with aluminum foil. Newspapers are porous, and the wax's color can seep through if spilled.
- If you spill wax, let it dry, then rub the spot with an ice cube. This will freeze the wax and allow you to easily scrape it off with a knife.
- Wax is a flammable material. Never leave it unattended on the stove, even if you are using a double boiler.

MOLDS

The typical way to create a candle is to use a mold—a container into which you insert the wick, pour the wax, cool the wax, and remove the shaped candle.

Many containers are permanent (glasses, bowls, ceramic or metal forms, and so on). With these, the candle does not need to be extracted. Leaving the candle in a container, however, causes the wax to lose the opalescence and shine it would have if it were removed. Using molds allows you to create a greater variety of candle projects.

Molds can be divided into two types:
- **Store-bought molds.** These molds are specifically constructed for making candles and are sold in a variety of shapes. They are convenient and, if used correctly, provide such excellent results that they quickly pay for themselves.
- **Homemade molds.** You can use any number of household containers to make candles. With a little creativity, these containers can yield inexpensive, unique, and beautiful candles.

Using Store-Bought Molds

Store-bought molds made of rigid, smooth-surfaced plastic can be found in most craft centers. They often come equipped with a candle-making needle.

1 Pass the wick through the hole in the bottom of the mold, then make a large knot on the end of the wick so it will plug the hole and hold in the wax. Stretch the wick to the top of the mold and tie the end to the needle. Support the needle on the top rim of the mold so the wick remains stiff and centered.

2 Heat the wax in a double boiler and pour it slowly into the mold. This type of mold usually has a kind of raised foot that allows it to remain steady during pouring.

3 Allow the wax to dry for 3 or 4 hours (longer for large molds), then cut off the knot at the bottom of the mold and remove the candle. Unwrap and trim the wick.

Rubber Molds for Embossed Candles

Malleable rubber molds are perfect for making elegant candles. They are a little more expensive than rigid molds, but they allow you to create stunning textures.

1 Pierce the tip of the mold, then pass the wick through it and knot it at the bottom. Hold the wick stiff and wrap the other end around the needle supported on the top rim. Put the mold into a drinking glass or other suitable container so it will remain vertical, then slowly pour the melted wax into it.

2 Let it cool for 4 or 5 hours, then trim the wick and remove the needle. Extract the candle by gently peeling back the rubber mold from the top, turning it inside out.

3 To give your candle an antique appearance, you can wipe a soft cloth dipped in brown shoe polish over its surface.

Plastic Molds for Silhouette Candles

You can buy these silhouette candle molds in craft centers at relatively low prices (they are also used to make soaps and shapes from modeling clay). Such molds are useful for making place-holder or floating candles.

1 Heat the wax in a double boiler and pour it into the mold until it reaches the mold's top. Allow the wax to cool for about 30 minutes—until it is solid, but not completely hard.

2 Remove the wax form and place it on a square of aluminum foil used to protect the work area.

TIPS AND TRICKS

- To more easily extract candles from molds, put them in the freezer for 15 minutes after they have cooled and are solid.
- To clean the molds, soak them in an old pot filled with hot water for a few minutes. Then quickly wipe them with a paper towel or dry cloth.
- In order to retain the form of the rubber molds, dust them with a little talcum powder and place a balled-up cloth inside each one.

3 Cut a piece of waxed wick, heat the tip of a needle, and make a hole through the center of the candle. Quickly insert the wick into the hole. The wax will mold itself around the wick to secure it.

4 These candles burn quickly. Make sure they are on a plate or other non-flammable surface before you light them.

HOMEMADE MOLDS

An inexpensive way to create candles is to use molds made from containers found around your house, such as cake and cookie molds, plastic bottles, or aluminum cans.

The method for using homemade molds is very similar to that of using store-bought molds. With homemade molds, you don't need to worry about cleaning or storing them—simply throw them away. It only takes a little imagination to find new forms, and you will save not only money, but also time and space.

Soda Cans

These are the simplest and most inexpensive molds to use for creating cylindrical candles. The concave bottom of the can creates an ideal indentation for the top of the finished candle.

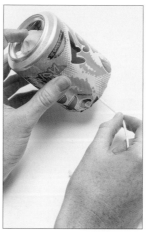

1 Pierce the bottom of the can using a hammer and nail. With a pair of sharp scissors, cut off the top of the can, being careful not to cut yourself (wear gloves). A good way to protect your hands when you're done cutting is to cover the sharp edge with masking tape.

2 Thread the wick through the hole at the bottom of the can. Make a knot in the wick, and cover the hole with a small ball of modeling clay to ensure the wax doesn't leak. Knot the opposite end of the wick to a needle or skewer so it remains centered.

3 Keep the can upright and pour in the melted wax. Let it dry 3 to 4 hours, untie the bottom knot, and remove the candle. Trim the wick to an appropriate height. This kind of candle is ideal for decorating with leaves or flowers, or in a thousand other ways.

Plastic Bottles

All shapes and sizes of plastic bottles can be used for candles and then simply thrown out.

1 Cut a plastic water bottle to the desired height, using the bottom half as your mold. Pierce the bottom with a large nail.

2 Insert the wick through the hole and seal the hole with a small ball of modeling clay. Pull the wick through the length of the bottle and affix the other end to a needle. Place the bottle in a bowl so it doesn't shift while you're filling it. Pour melted wax into the bottle, being careful not to move the wick.

3 Let dry for at least 4 hours before you remove the candle. To make this process easier, use scissors to make several small cuts around the top edge of the bottle. You can then peel the plastic away from the candle. Trim the wick to an appropriate height.

Metal Cake and Cookie Molds

Little cookie molds, found in kitchen and pastry shops, are particularly handy for creating floating candles.

1 Heat the wax in a double boiler and pour it slowly into the mold. Let it dry for 15 minutes, which should be sufficient for a small mold. Do not allow the wax to harden completely.

2 Cut a waxed wick into as many pieces as you have candles. Push the wick through the center of the candle to the bottom. The wax will quickly shape itself around the wick.

3 Let the wax cool for 1 hour before you remove the candle. Place the candle on a plate or other nonflammable surface before burning. These are also perfect as floating candles.

GEL CANDLES

Gel candles have become very popular in recent years. Store-bought gel wax looks like a transparent or translucent goo and can be melted just like regular wax, but once it solidifies, it remains transparent.

The transparency of gel wax allows you to make candles containing interesting objects, from flowers to fruits to small gifts. The gel is practical—it is easily removed from molds and, once solid, doesn't drip. Gel wax is more expensive than standard wax flakes or granules, however. You can purchase uncolored wax and add your own color with food coloring or buy already-colored wax. Some gel wax comes in a tube and doesn't need to be melted—you just put it in a container and insert the wick. If you do need to melt the wax, you can do so in a double boiler or in a microwave-safe bowl heated in a microwave on high for 2 to 3 minutes (time will vary according to the quantity of wax). Just don't bring the wax to a boil.

You can also melt used gel wax candles to remove the inserted objects and reuse the wax to make new candles—the new ones won't be as transparent as they were when they were first created, but they can still be quite attractive.

Basic Preparation

1 Slowly melt the gel wax in a double boiler on medium heat (or in a microwave) to avoid forming bubbles. When the wax is completely melted, add a few drops of scented oil to perfume the candle.

2 Pour the melted gel into a glass or other clear container.

3 Let the wax solidify for about 20 minutes, then insert the wick, making sure it's perfectly centered.

Gel Candle with an Object

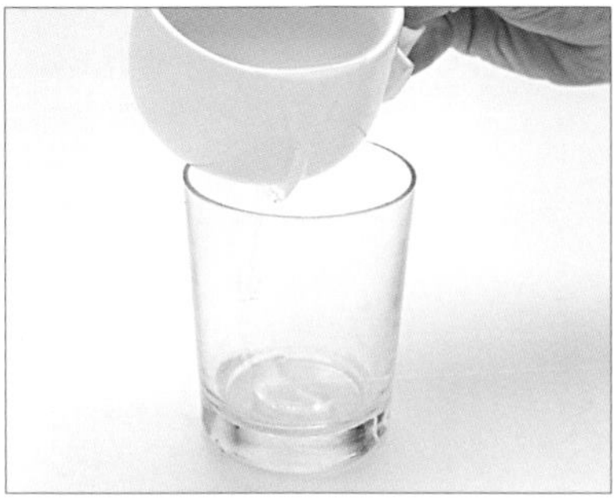

1 Heat the wax in a double boiler until it is completely melted, then slowly pour it into a glass container of your choosing, creating a base approximately 1 to 1½ inches high on which to place the object.

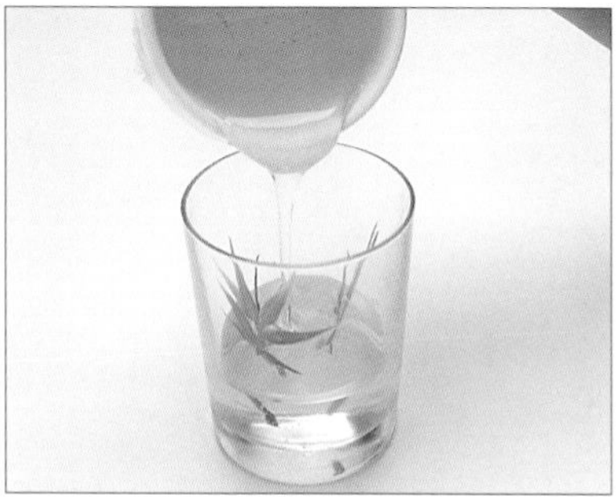

2 Allow the wax to partially solidify, then arrange your chosen objects, pushing them down about ⅛ inch into the wax. Cover the objects with more melted wax until it is about 1 inch from the top of the container.

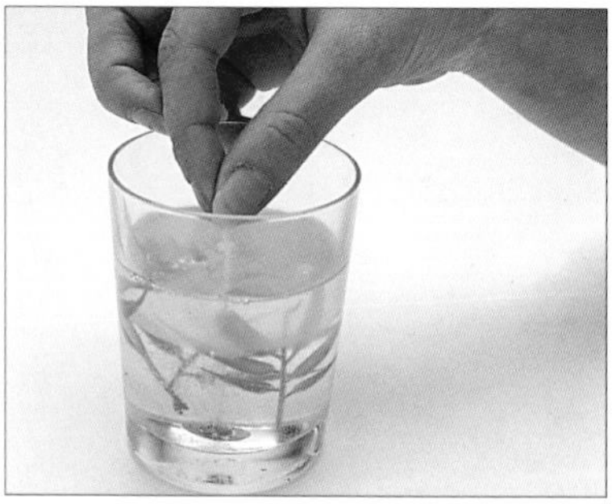

3 Let the wax cool for approximately 20 minutes and insert the wick. Make sure the wick is stiff and centered so the candle will burn evenly.

Layering Candles with Wax and Gel

To create a particularly interesting effect, you can layer regular wax with gel wax. Although you need to wait for each layer to solidify completely before adding the next, the results are well worth the effort.

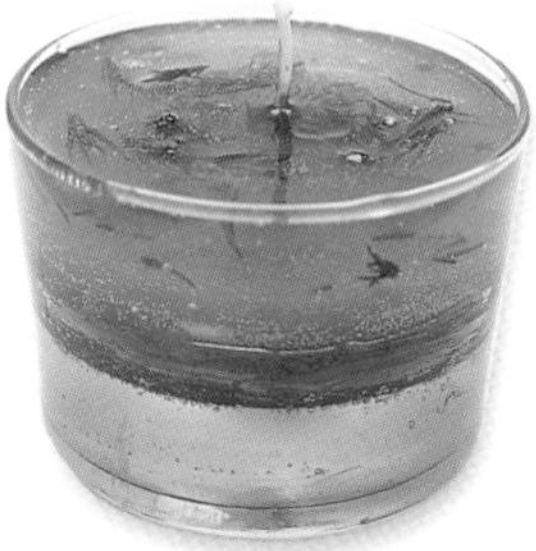

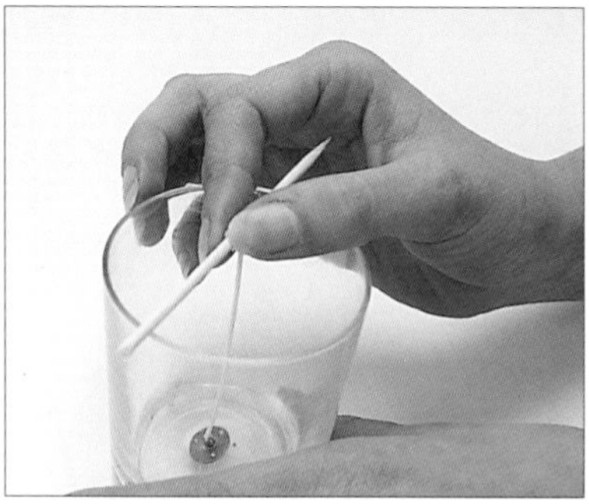

1 Cut a waxed wick so it is an inch or two higher than the container and knot the end around a skewer. Support the stick on either edge of the container so the wick remains stiff and centered.

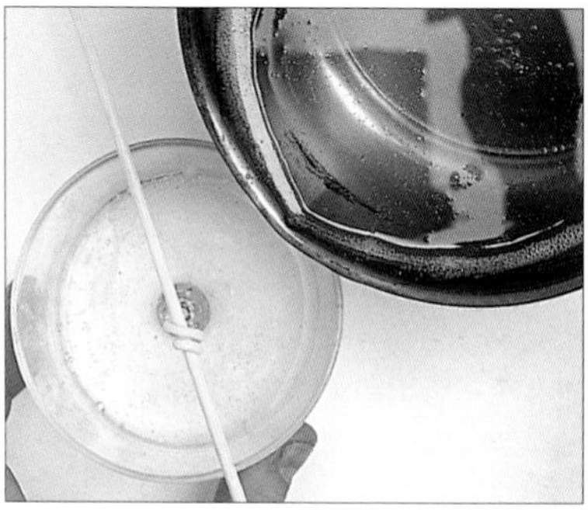

2 Melt the gel wax in a double boiler. When the wax is completely melted, slowly pour it into the container, making a gel layer approximately 2 inches high. Let this layer solidify.

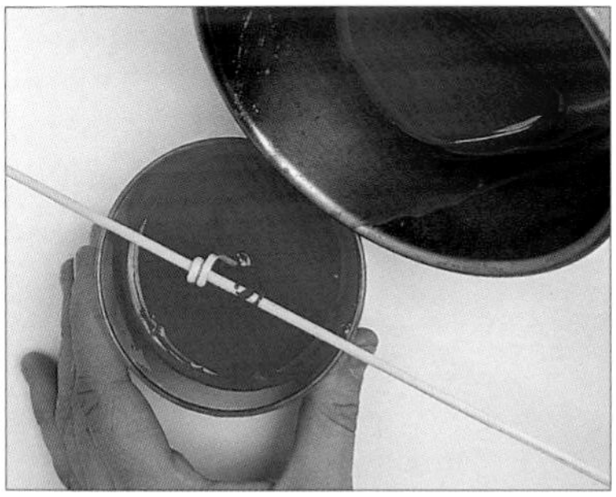

3 Melt a solid, colorful wax in a double boiler and pour a layer approximately 1 inch high on top of the gel. Allow it to solidify.

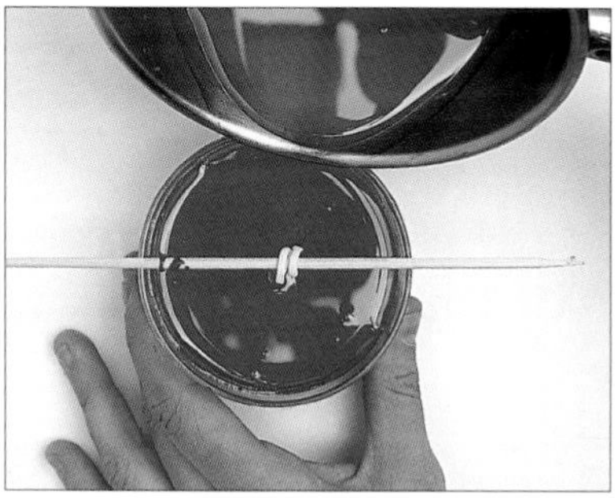

4 Create a third layer with colored transparent gel. Let this layer solidify.

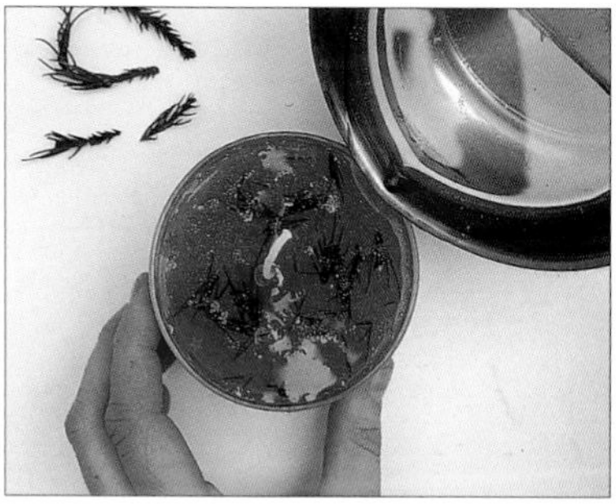

5 Complete the candle with a final layer of gel—yellow is used here, and dried pine needles were added. Trim the wick to an appropriate height.

Projects

Orange Candle

These aromatic candles are reminiscent of winter in the Mediterranean. The stimulating and harmonizing characteristics of the citrus are diffused by the heat of the flame. Great for freshening any room, they are especially useful in the kitchen to soften the smells of cooking.

As Gifts

These candles make wonderful gifts. An elegant way to present one is to wrap it in transparent acetate paper (such as that used by a florist) and knot it with a green cord to which you have tied dried pieces of orange. Prepare the pieces by cutting slices at least ½ inch thick and drying them for 30 minutes on a cloth, then warm them in an oven set at a low temperature (120°F) for 8 to 10 hours.

To Make the Candles

Materials

- 4 large oranges
- 17 ½ oz paraffin flakes and stearin (10 parts wax, 1 part stearin)
- Orange wax crayon
- Orange-scented oil
- Waxed wicks

Equipment

- Double boiler
- Spoon
- Kitchen knife
- Skewer

Note: For this and any other candle—if you don't have a premade wick, you can create one by dipping a cotton cord in melted wax.

HINT

These delicious candles can be made with all kinds of citrus fruits. Trust your instincts and your nose to create personalized candles: a mandarin orange that smells like lemon, a grapefruit with the fragrance of bergamot, an orange scented like cedar . . .

1 Select a large orange with a uniform round shape. Using a sharp knife, cut off the top of the orange, making sure the cut is straight all the way around.

2 Using a teaspoon and the knife, remove all the pulp from the orange. Clean it out carefully while making sure not to break the peel—this would make it unusable. Rinse the orange with cold water and let it dry.

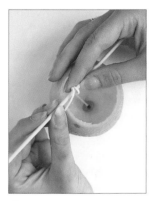

3 Wrap the tip of the wick around a skewer. Support the skewer on the top edge of the orange so the wick remains suspended in the center and touches the bottom. Prepare four oranges in this manner.

4 Melt the paraffin and stearin mixture in a double boiler. Add orange coloring and 12 drops of orange-scented oil, increasing the number of drops if you want a stronger scent. While the wax is melting, stir it with a skewer or spoon to ensure there are no lumps and the color is consistent.

5 When the wax is completely melted and colored, slowly pour it into one of the emptied oranges, being especially careful not to move the wick, which must remain centered. Let the candle cool until the wax is thoroughly hardened. Untie the wick and trim. Follow the same steps to create the other three candles.

19

Pomegranate Candle

Here's a surprising combination:
Is it a candle or a pomegranate?
Actually, it's a little of both. Made
from two carved pomegranates,
these candles are filled with
irregular wax shapes. The wax is
scented with peach to create a
pleasing combination of the two
fruits, making these candles ideal
for use as a centerpiece.

An Alternative

You can make an elegant display with this candle by adding a ring of autumn decorations around the bottom, such as fabric leaves, corn, gourds, and so on. Perfect for a romantic dinner for two, or, for a formal meal, you can create a centerpiece using whole or open pomegranates combined with the pomegranate candles. The result is sure to impress.

To Make the Candles

Materials

- 3 ½ oz gold wax granules
- 2 large pomegranates
- Peach-scented oil
- Waxed wick
- Red water-based spray paint

Equipment

- Kitchen knife
- Bowl
- Spoon
- Paper towel
- Newspaper
- Skewer
- Scissors

1 Using a knife, slice a thin, quarter-sized circle from the peel on one side of the pomegranate. This will serve as the candle's base.

2 Make two cuts in the pomegranate from end to end, approximately 2 inches from each other in the middle, then remove the wedge-shaped slice from the fruit.

3 Remove all the seeds from the fruit with a spoon and thoroughly dry the shell with a paper towel.

HINT

To ensure that the pomegranates last a long time, dry them first. Scoop out all the inner fruit and seeds and place a balled-up paper towel inside each of the shells.

Place the pomegranates in the oven at a low temperature (not above 120°F). Change the paper towel every 2 hours, repeating this process 3 or 4 times, allowing the pomegranates to dry for approximately 6 hours.

4 In a well-ventilated area, spread gold wax granules on a newspaper and spray lightly with the red spray paint (make sure to use water-based paint). Let the granules dry completely, then place them in a bowl and add 4 drops of peach-scented oil.

5 Stir the wax granules to disperse the peach fragrance, then use a spoon to fill each of the empty pomegranate shells with the wax.

6 Cut a piece of waxed wick approximately 3 or 4 inches long. Use a skewer to make a small passage through the wax granules, then insert the wick through the center. Make the second candle the same way.

21

Vanilla Candle
in a Coconut Shell

These scented candles will remind you of a
tropical beach and add an exotic breeze to any
room. The vanilla candle, warm and sweet, is
perfect for creating a relaxed atmosphere.

An Alternative

You can use similar materials to create a Zen-inspired centerpiece. Use the coconut shell as a candleholder and line the bottom with small pebbles or sand, then place a vanilla-scented pillar in the center. Use smooth stones to create a base for the candleholder, and decorate with tropical green leaves. Another quick and simple idea is to create a small lantern using the coconut shell: Carve a design into one half of the coconut shell, then place a tea light in the other half and cover with the carved shell to create an illuminated sphere.

To Make the Candles

Materials
- Aluminum foil
- Empty coconut shells
- 1 ¾ oz opaque white wax
- Waxed wick
- Vanilla-scented oil

Equipment
- Double boiler
- Needle
- Spoon

1 Form a small ball of aluminum foil and place it in the hole in the coconut shell to prevent the wax from leaking.

2 Melt opaque white wax in a double boiler over low heat, stirring constantly, and then pour a couple drops of wax into the coconut shell to test the aluminum foil plug. Add 3 or 4 drops of vanilla-scented oil to the wax and stir to disperse the fragrance.

HINT

To obtain two coconut shells, drill into the bottom of a store-bought coconut, drain the milk, and cut the coconut in half with a hacksaw. Then remove the inner pulp with a knife.

3 Gently pour the wax into the coconut shell until it is approximately ½ inch from the top.

4 Before the wax is completely hardened, make a hole in its center with a needle and insert the waxed wick. Let cool.

Halloween Candle

Celebrate Halloween by putting these candles on your windowsill or alongside your jack-o'-lantern. Empty the gourds and fill with orange wax to make a simple seasonal candle. The mild vanilla fragrance, warm and slightly sweet, adds to the enchanted atmosphere of the most haunted night of the year.

An Alternative

Make your gourds even more eerie by turning them into little witches. With a black felt-tipped marker, draw eyes on a gourd, then add a witch's hat made of green tissue paper shaped into a cone with a circle of construction paper as a base. Decorate the hat using gold ribbon.

How, When, Where

Use these luminous gourds at a Halloween party, arranged on a tray as a centerpiece. Or use them as placeholders by writing each guest's name on a candle with a felt-tipped marker.

To Make the Candle

Materials

- Small gourd
- 3 ½ oz opaque white wax
- Red candle coloring
- Vanilla-scented oil
- Waxed wick

Equipment

- Double boiler
- Scissors
- Craft knife
- Needle
- Spoon

1 With the knife, cut off the top of the gourd and remove all pulp and seeds from inside using a spoon and knife.

2 Melt the wax in a double boiler over low heat and add 4 drops of red coloring and 5 drops of vanilla-scented oil. Stir until color and scent are dispersed.

HINT

Be careful to remove all the pulp from the gourd; if a piece remains attached to the rind, it will rot the candle. Turn the emptied gourd upside down to dry completely before filling it with wax.

3 Carefully pour the wax into the empty gourd, filling it until the wax is about ½ inch from the top. Let cool until partially solid.

4 Pierce a hole in the center of the candle with a needle and insert the waxed wick. Cool until hardened.

Bell Pepper Lantern

You need only a little talent and imagination to turn bell peppers into lanterns, perfect for a fun dinner with friends. Empty a large pepper, carve a creative design, and place a lemon-scented basket of pebbles and tea light in its center. The light will shine through the pepper, casting elegant patterns onto the table and dispersing the sharp aromas of lemon and pepper.

An Alternative

A new way to interpret the classic jack-o'-lantern is to use a carved bell pepper in its place. Create a glowing center-piece or intersperse red and yellow peppers as place-holders to grin at each of your guests.

How, When, Where

Arrange these lanterns on a tray covered with green leaves to contrast with the red and yellow of the peppers. Decorate with other vegetables of your choice to create a stunning centerpiece perfect for a vegetarian dinner.

To Make the Lanterns

Materials

- 1 large, firm red pepper
- 2 large, firm yellow peppers
- 3 tea lights
- 3 baskets to fit inside the peppers
- Small pebbles
- Lemon-scented oil

Equipment

- Large, flat plate
- Craft knife
- Spoon

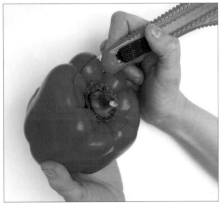

1 With the knife blade held at an angle, cut around the stem of a pepper and remove the top.

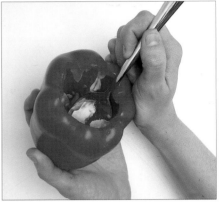

2 Use a spoon to remove the pepper's seeds, and scrape the inside to remove any dangling threads.

HINT

Be careful when emptying the pepper to be sure you don't scrape too much skin from the inside. If it loses too much of its skin, the pepper will wilt from the candle's flame.

3 With the knife, carve designs into the skin, being sure to leave enough space so you can remove the shapes with your fingers. Use regular or irregular shapes to give the candle a distinctive appearance.

4 Fill the basket with small pebbles, then add a few drops of lemon-scented oil.

5 Place the basket inside the pepper and place a tea light on top of the pebbles. Repeat the process for the remaining peppers. Arrange the peppers on a flat plate to create a brilliant visual and aromatic display.

Citrus Candle

Welcome your guests with a beautifully arranged tray of citrus candles decorated with dried orange and lemon peels. The glowing light and intense citrus scent lend a pleasant atmosphere to any entranceway.

As Gifts

Make an elegant gift by wrapping a strip of textured paper scented with orange oil around one of these candles. Add a dried orange slice to one side and tie the package with naturally colored cord. To create a lemon-themed candle, use yellow textured paper and lemon-scented oil. You can also add a small sack of orange or lemon candies to the gift as an extra treat.

To Make the Candles

Materials

- 2 milk cartons with square bases
- 2 waxed wicks
- Orange and lemon-scented oils
- Paraffin wax flakes: 20 teaspoonfuls per candle
- Stearin for candles: 2 teaspoonfuls per candle
- Dried orange and lemon slices
- Orange and yellow wax crayons

Equipment

- Double boiler
- Craft knife
- Spoon
- Needle

HINT

Citrus fruits can easily be dried in a ventilated oven. Cut the fruit into slices and place on a tray in the oven for 8 to 10 hours at a temperature of approximately 105°F.

1 Melt the paraffin wax and stearin in a double boiler; after the mixture is completely melted, add one crumbled orange wax crayon. Stir the mixture until the color is consistent throughout. Add 8 drops of orange-scented oil.

2 Cut the top from a milk carton to make a mold approximately 4 inches high. Use a spoon to cover the inner sides of the carton with a thin layer of melted wax. Wait a few moments until the wax starts to solidify, then gently press a dried orange slice onto each side of the candle.

3 Fill the mold with melted wax until it is approximately 1 inch from the top, being careful not to detach the dried orange slices. Let the wax solidify for about 20 minutes.

4 Use a needle to make a hole through the center of the still-soft candle. Thread the wick into the hole. Allow the candle to dry at room temperature for about 12 hours.

5 Place the candle in the freezer for approximately 10 minutes, then gently tear the milk carton off the candle. Make the lemon-scented candle using the same process.

Mauve Flower Candle

Give yourself a relaxation break to enjoy the warm scent and glow of these mauve flower candles. They create an intimate atmosphere as they slowly release a sweet floral aroma—a perfect candle for those who love soft scents and relaxation.

As Gifts

Wrap the candle in burlap to emphasize its natural ingredients and allow the herbal scent to escape through the loose weave. Knot the package with a scented cord of fabric leaves to further accentuate the candle's organic essence.

How, When, Where

Mauve flowers are used by herbalists for their variety of healing properties. They are considered to be both a relaxant and a decongestant. Ancient Romans used mauve flowers to make warm compresses and in footbaths to soothe aching feet.

To Make the Candles

Materials

- 3 plastic bottles
- 3 waxed wicks
- Modeling clay
- Paraffin wax: 10 teaspoonfuls per candle
- Stearin: 1 teaspoonful per candle
- Dried mauve flowers: 3 teaspoonfuls per candle

Equipment

- Double boiler
- Craft knife
- Spoon
- Glass or similar container
- Needle

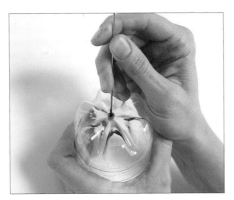

1 Cut the top off a plastic soda bottle, leaving the bottom portion the desired height of your candle. Using a sharp needle or nail, make a hole directly in the center of the bottle's bottom. The hole must be large enough to thread the wick, but not so large that wax will leak out.

2 Insert the wick through the hole and make a knot outside the bottle, leaving about 4 inches of extra length. Cover the knot with a ball of modeling clay so the wax doesn't leak.

HINT

As it solidifies, the wax may sink around the wick. This can compromise the stability of the candle, so you may need to add melted wax to fill in the depression when the candle is partially solid. Repeat if necessary.

3 Prop the bottle in a glass or small bowl so it will stay upright, then pull the wick to the top and tie it around a needle or skewer supported on the rim. Evenly distribute the dried mauve flowers on the bottom of the bottle.

4 Melt the paraffin wax and stearin in a double boiler at a low temperature. Pour the melted wax into the bottle and let it harden completely. Before removing the candle, place the mold in the refrigerator for a few minutes. Remove the clay and trim the bottom knot and top wick.

Vanilla Candle with Coffee Beans

Use these candles to turn your veranda into a Parisian café, or to enhance the ambiance of a Sunday morning as you curl up with a cup of coffee. The vanilla essence, a warm and intense scent, complements the sharp aroma of the coffee beans.

As Gifts

Take a piece of white tulle or burlap and glue coffee beans to it randomly or in a pattern. Let the glue dry for about a half hour, then wrap the candle inside the fabric and tie it with a raffia ribbon.

An Alternative

An inexpensive way to create these candles is to use plastic bottles, cut about 6 inches from the bottom, for molds. You can choose high, narrow bottles, or use short, square cartons to create a variety of shapes.

To Make the Candle

Materials
- 17 oz white paraffin flakes
- 1 1/2 oz stearin
- Waxed wick
- A few handfuls of whole coffee beans
- Vanilla-scented oil

Equipment
- Double boiler
- Spoon
- Skewer
- Cylindrical plastic candle mold

1 Prepare the wax mixture by combining the paraffin flakes with the stearin. In a double boiler, melt the mixture, then add 8 drops of vanilla-scented oil and stir.

2 Insert the wick through the base of the cylindrical mold and knot it at the bottom so the wax doesn't leak out. To ensure the wick remains in the center, wrap the other end around a skewer balanced on the mold's rim.

3 Pour a handful of coffee beans on the bottom of the mold, then cover them with the melted wax until it reaches one-third the height of the cylinder. Allow the wax to cool for about 10 minutes.

HINT

Serve your guests coffee on a tray decorated with these candles, adding a vanilla bean to the sugar bowl to flavor the sugar. This ancient custom comes from Polynesia.

4 Add another handful of coffee beans and fill another one-third of the mold with melted wax. Allow to cool for 10 minutes, then repeat the process once more until you have filled the entire mold.

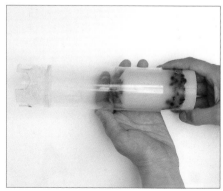

5 Let the candle cool for approximately 12 hours at room temperature. Then place the mold in the freezer for 10 minutes, after which you can remove the finished candle from the mold.

Green Apple Candle

Create a stylish and aromatic decoration with a green apple candle covered with fabric leaves and perched on a chic wrought-iron candleholder. The candle burns slowly, releasing a pleasantly fresh scent. The energizing properties will create an atmosphere perfect for both entertaining and spending quality family time.

As Gifts

Play off the brilliant shade of the green apple to create a simple yet lovely gift. Take a green cardboard box of a suitable size to hold the candle and cover the bottom with a handful of green sand. Then carefully place the candle on top. Decorate the inside and outside of the box by gluing fabric leaves to the cardboard.

Another Idea

The green apple scent can be complemented with chamomile; the term *chamomile,* in fact, is derived from the Greek word meaning "similar to the apple" because the two scents are so alike. You can therefore create a candle of whatever shape and color you choose and add a few drops of chamomile-scented oil. These two candles, when lighted together, will produce a signature scent that could not be achieved with just one.

To Make the Candle

Materials

- Strand of fabric leaves
- Wrought-iron candle-holder
- Candle glue
- Green apple candle

Equipment

- Scissors
- Cotton cloth
- Hot glue gun
- Small paintbrush

1 Using scissors, cut the fabric leaves off at their bases, eliminating the plastic vine.

2 Clean the candleholder with a cotton cloth, then line its inner edge with glue drops using a hot glue gun, removing any remaining glue threads.

HINT

There is a simple way to remove residual wax from candle holders without resorting to messy cleaning products or trying to melt the wax off. Place the candle holder in the freezer for a few minutes; the wax can then be removed with a spatula or a knife.

3 Before the glue hardens, position the leaves in a circle along the edge so that their tips are slightly protruding and their edges overlap. Secure the leaves by pressing down lightly with your fingertips.

4 Take five additional leaves and, using your scissors, cut a small leaf shape from the center of each fabric leaf.

5 With a small paintbrush, spread a thin layer of candle glue on the back of each of these leaves, and position them on top of the candle, encircling the wick in the shape of a flower. Brush another thin layer of glue on top of the five leaves, being careful not to cover the wick.

Herb Pot Candle

Create a warm and soothing atmosphere on your patio with these candles made entirely of natural materials. The terra-cotta pots are wrapped with raffia ribbon, which secures the leaves. Scented with lemon, sage, and bay, these candles add a refreshing aroma to any spring evening.

As Gifts

The way these candles are made allows for easy gift giving. From a sheet of sturdy paper, cut three rectangles approximately 2½ by 1½ inches, and neatly write one candle scent on each. Glue the tags to small wooden sticks. Cut each stick until it is the correct height to be used as a flag in the terra-cotta pot. To insert the stick, it's important that the wax is not completely hardened, so you should create your flags ahead of time.

To Make the Candles

Materials

- 3 small terra-cotta pots
- 3 waxed wicks
- Lemon, sage, and bay-scented oils
- 5 oz prepared green wax (enough to make all 3 candles)
- Lemon, sage, and bay leaves
- Raffia ribbon
- Modeling clay

Equipment

- Double boiler
- Spoon
- Scissors
- Needle

1 Melt 1½ ounces of wax in a double boiler over low heat, stirring often. The wax should not get so hot that it forms bubbles. Add 5 drops of bay-scented oil and stir to disperse.

2 Cover the hole on the bottom of the terra-cotta pot with a ball of modeling clay to prevent the wax from leaking.

3 Pour a few drops of melted wax in the bottom of the pot and wait until it solidifies. This creates a strong layer upon which to pour the remaining wax. Fill the pot with the rest of the melted wax until it's approximately ½ inch from the top.

HINT

Create a place to arrange your aromatic grass candles using other natural materials. Take a rattan or bamboo placemat, lay down a few tropical leaves, and you have a clever display.

4 When the wax is partially solid and has formed a dull patina on top, insert a needle to the bottom of the vase and insert the waxed wick. Allow to harden for several hours, then trim the wick to the desired height.

5 Place a bay leaf on the side of the vase and spray it with glue, then tie a raffia ribbon around the vase, making a bow over the leaf. Repeat this process for the lemon and sage candles.

Multicolored Cinnamon Candle

Many different layers and colors make up these classic candles, and they can be adapted to brighten any room of your house, from the kitchen to the office. Cinnamon saturates the room with its characteristically intense and warm fragrance.

As Gifts

Continue the layering theme to create the gift wrap for this candle. Wrap the candle in white tissue paper, then cover the package with a variety of brightly colored materials and colors, securing them in the center with orange string. Or cover the candle with tissue paper and tie varying lengths and colors of wool thread from the base to the top.

To Make the Candles

Materials

- 1 oz turquoise wax
- 1 oz maroon wax
- 1 oz yellow wax
- 1 oz olive wax
- 1 oz army green wax
- 1 oz bottle green wax
- 1 oz brown wax
- 2 waxed wicks
- Cinnamon-scented oil

Equipment

- Double boiler
- Spoon
- Scissors
- Needle
- Rigid plastic cup
- Shorter plastic mold

1 Melt turquoise wax in a double boiler over low heat, then add 3 or 4 drops of cinnamon-scented oil.

2 Make a hole in the bottom of the plastic cup and thread the wick through the bottom, making a knot to prevent the wax from leaking out. Hold the wick vertical by wrapping the other end around a needle supported on the cup's rim.

3 Pour the turquoise wax into the cup, creating a layer about 1 inch high. Allow to cool completely.

4 Repeat steps 1 and 3 for the remaining layers, pouring first the melted and scented yellow wax, then olive, army green, bottle green, brown, and, finally, maroon. Before pouring each layer, make sure the previous layer has cooled completely or the colors will run together.

5 When all the layers have cooled, trim the wick to the desired height. Gently press on the sides and bottom of the cup to remove the candle. To make the other candle, use a shorter mold and vary the colors to your liking.

Fruit Jar Candle

For a bright and modern kitchen, decorate with these fruity candles. The clear jars reveal the intensely colored wax, scented with orange, lemon, and strawberry. The fresh aromas create an inviting atmosphere in which to gather with friends.

An Alternative

For a child's birthday party, decorate these fruity candles with multicolored soft pompoms—you need to add only a drop of glue to each pompom to secure them to the jar. You can also use the candles as place-holders and party favors. (Be sure to tell each child's parents that you are sending them home with a candle to avoid glass breakage or a fire hazard.)

To Make the Candles

Materials
- 3 small glass jars
- 3 waxed wicks
- Strawberry, lemon, and orange-scented oils
- Prepared candle wax, 2 oz per candle
- Pink, yellow, and orange wax crayons

Equipment
- Double boiler
- Spoon
- Needle

1 Melt 2 ounces of wax in a double boiler over low heat, making sure it does not reach the boiling point. When the wax is completely melted, add 3 drops of strawberry-scented oil and stir carefully.

2 Add a piece of pink wax crayon to the melted wax, crumbling it with your fingers so it dissolves easily. Stir the wax until the pink crayon is melted and the color is consistent throughout.

HINT

If the wax begins to sink as it hardens, add more melted wax to the jar, repeating the process if necessary.

3 Pour the wax into a clear jar until it reaches the top; let cool for approximately 1 hour.

4 When the wax is partially solid, use a needle to pierce a hole to the bottom of the jar and insert the waxed wick. Allow to cool completely, then trim the wick to the desired height. Make the other candles by using yellow and orange wax crayons and adding lemon and orange-scented oils.

Cocoa Candle

The strong and sweet scent of this candle enhances a warm evening shared with friends. The vintage tin gives the candle a particularly appealing look, perfect for chocolate gourmets or anyone who loves a delicious fragrance.

As Gifts

Use a piece of slightly crumpled tissue paper or rice paper to package this candle: Wrap the can inside the paper, tying the top with a piece of blue ribbon. Thread a couple of seashells on the ribbon for a finishing touch.

How, When, Where

The blue color, inviting meditation and physical regeneration, makes this the perfect bathroom candle. Place the candle on the edge of the bathtub to give your bath a pleasant glow. Bath salts with a sea-inspired scent complete the atmosphere.

To Make the Candle

Materials

- 10 oz opaque blue wax
- Cylindrical can with silver finish
- Maritime pine oil
- Approximately 25 inches blue cord
- Mother-of-pearl shell

Equipment

- Double boiler
- Spoon
- Skewer
- Glue

1 Melt the blue wax in a double boiler over low heat, stirring constantly, and add a few drops of maritime pine oil.

2 Insert a waxed wick into the center of the can, fastening its tip around a skewer balanced on the can's rim.

3 Pour the melted wax into the can, being careful not to bump the wick from the center. Let cool completely.

HINT

Cylindrical silver cans can be found in craft centers. You can also use any silver tins you find around your home, such as those that sometimes hold elegant bath products. Simply wash out any leftover residue and remove the labels.

4 Wrap the blue cord around the can several times, keeping the cord in the middle, then tie the loose ends in a knot.

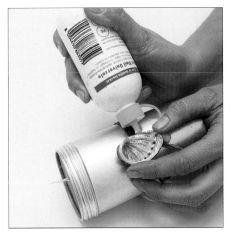

5 Glue the mother-of-pearl shell to the cord's knot, pressing down for a few seconds to secure it.

Beeswax Flower Candle

These small candles are made to "flower" from beeswax sheets. Natural beeswax gives off a sweet, calming honey scent; the imaginative form and relaxing aroma make these candles perfect for easing children into dreamland— just make sure to blow them out before you leave the room.

An Alternative

Arrange six small beeswax votives in a wicker basket with a flat base and attach a few resin bees to the candles and around the edge of the basket. You will then have a wonderful arrangement to place on a family room table where everyone can enjoy its pleasant scent.

How, When, Where

Liven up a dinner party by making a small candle for each guest. Write each guest's name on parchment paper, glue the tag to the candle's stalk, and place one at each setting.

To Make the Candles

Materials
- 7 natural beeswax sheets
- Waxed wicks
- 1 bag of resin bees with pins*

Equipment
- Craft knife
- Pen or pencil
- Sheet of drawing paper
- Scissors

You can usually find these at craft centers in the candle or flower section.

Pattern for flower

HINT

Beeswax candles can attract insects so it's best not to use them while dining out on your patio or near your garden.

1 Take three sheets of beeswax, place them on top of one another, and use a knife to cut them in half lengthwise. You will then have six equal-sized wax strips.

2 Place a wax strip on a clean work area and lay a wick along one edge, leaving 1 to 1½ inches of the wick's tip overhanging. Slowly begin to roll the wax around the wick.

3 Roll the strip until you reach the other side and fasten the edge by applying slight pressure with your fingertips. Prepare six more candles using these steps.

4 Draw a five-petaled flower outline on a piece of paper to use as a stencil. You will need twelve flowers total, so your outline should be sized to cut three flowers from each of the four remaining beeswax sheets.

5 Take two beeswax flowers and lay one on top of the other, staggering the petals so there are no spaces between. Lightly press them together in the center. Gently fasten the flowers to the candle's base.

6 Mold the petals with your fingers so they are slightly raised around the base. Decorate each of the candles with the resin bees.

Beeswax Sunflower Candle

These glass "sunflowers" are lovely
accompaniments to a centerpiece
of real sunflowers. The clear gel allows
a glimpse into the beeswax base, while
bees buzz atop the petals. The sweet
beeswax fragrance is further enhanced
by the clean, citrus scent of ginestra.

An Alternative

You can also make several small candles with bees enclosed in the gel. Fill a small round glass with clear gel wax, then insert the wick and the bees. Add another bee and a small piece of beeswax to the edge of the glass for decoration.

As Gifts

To wrap one of these sunflowers, lay down a sheet of clear cellophane and cover with a circle of yellow tissue paper. Place a wineglass on top of the circle, and lift the paper up around the glass. Tie with a piece of yellow ribbon, and glue a bee to the package as an extra touch.

To Make the Candles

Materials
- Wineglass
- Cognac glass
- 7 oz clear gel wax
- Ginestra-scented oil
- Beeswax sheet
- 2 craft beehives
- 4 craft bees
- 2 waxed wicks

Equipment
- Double boiler
- Spoon
- Skewer
- Craft knife
- Sheet of drawing paper
- Scissors
- Pen or pencil

Pattern for sunflower petals

HINT

After cutting the petals, do not handle them too much as your body heat can soften and deform the wax. If this happens, place the beeswax in the refrigerator for a few minutes.

1 Cube the gel wax and add a few drops of ginestra-scented oil, then melt in a double boiler over low heat, stirring constantly.

2 Pour 1 to 1½ inches of melted wax into the wineglass, then insert the beehive base, pushing it toward the bottom of the glass with a skewer. Fill the glass with melted wax.

3 Before the wax hardens completely, insert the wick, centering it above the beehive base. Allow it to solidify.

4 Using the pattern, cut out two differently sized paper stencils. Then place the outlines on the beeswax sheets and cut out twenty petals: ten of each size.

5 Press the wax petals against the glass, slightly overlapping them, alternating the two sizes, then shape the petals with your fingers.

6 Trim the wire on each of the bees to approximately 1 inch, then place two of the bees on different petals. Create the cognac glass sunflower in the same way.

51

Beeswax Calla Lily Candle

Beeswax sheets are magically transformed
into a bouquet of calla lily candles. The
warm honey fragrance makes these
the perfect candles to light a
romantic dinner or sweeten
a Sunday breakfast.

As Gifts

For an elegant and heart-felt gift, wrap one of these candles in florist's paper, just as you would a real flower. Wrap red raffia ribbon around the stem and add a red bow to the corner for the final touch.

How, When, Where

Invite your friends to an afternoon tea. The relaxing honey fragrance from the calla lily bouquet will create a relaxing ambiance for long conversation while you serve honey-flavored scones to delight the tastebuds.

To Make the Candles

Materials

- 3 beeswax sheets
- 4 wooden dowels approximately 12 inches long
- Waxed wicks
- Green florist's tape

Equipment

- Scissors
- Craft knife
- Sheet of drawing paper
- Pen or pencil

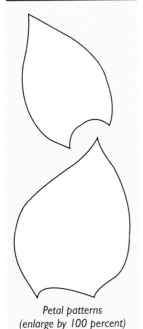

Petal patterns (enlarge by 100 percent)

1 Cut a strip of beeswax, approximately 5 × 2 inches, from one of the sheets, then lay a 3-inch wick along one edge, leaving 1 inch of the wick overhanging.

2 Lay a wooden dowel alongside the wick, and then tightly roll the beeswax to fully enclose the dowel and the wick.

3 Use the patterns, and cut four calla lily petals from the beeswax sheets.

4 Choose one, and soften the wax with your fingers, gently pressing just inside the edge of the petal to create a slight thickness around the border.

5 Wrap the petal's base around the beeswax rod you made in step 2, applying pressure with your fingers to attach it.

6 Wrap green florist's tape around the base of the wax pistil and petal and down the entire stem; lightly moisten at the base to fasten. Repeat this process to make three more candles.

53

Beeswax Lemon Candle

Here is a simple way to use small candles to create a lemon-inspired centerpiece. Because beeswax is so malleable, you can use it to create a variety of shapes. The sharp lemon scent provides a unique contrast to the sweet honey fragrance of the beeswax.

An Alternative

Create any kind of fruit you like using beeswax. You can make a pear by first molding the beeswax into an oval shape, then covering it with additional strips so it is thicker at the bottom and narrows to a "stem" at the top. Use a similar process to create an apple, adding a beeswax leaf at the top.

How, When, Where

Add a beeswax fruit plate to dinner with friends: Create several small beeswax fruit candles and place them on a decorative plate to use as a centerpiece. The warm candle glow and sweet honey fragrance create an inviting atmosphere.

To Make the Candles

Materials
- Beeswax sheets
- 3 waxed wicks
- Artificial leaves

Equipment
- Scissors
- Matches or lighter

HINT

To make wrapping the wax strips easier, use your fingers to slightly heat the wax until it is soft and flexible.

1 Using the knife, cut a strip of beeswax from the sheet approximately 2 inches long.

2 Lay a waxed wick along the long edge of the sheet and roll the wax until the wick is completely enclosed.

3 Cut several wax strips a little wider than 1 inch each. Wrap the strips around the wick in irregular patterns until you have created an oval shape.

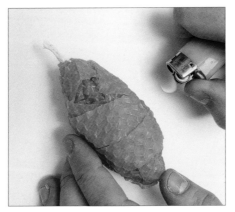

4 Use a lit match or lighter to warm the beeswax, being careful to not get the flame too close, until the wax strips are molded together.

5 Attach additional slightly heated strips to the form until you achieve the size and shape of a lemon. Repeat the process to create two more lemons. Garnish your centerpiece with artificial leaves.

Tea Time Candle

Unique conversation pieces, these candles will brighten the 5 o'clock hour, traditional tea time. A clear glass is turned into a cup of tea with a tea bag, a dried orange slice, and honey-scented wax. The wafers are made with beeswax and yellow and brown wax sheets, layered to create a gourmet delicacy for the eyes and nose.

An Alternative

Make several small dessert candles using a base of clear gel wax. Use red and orange coloring for strawberry and apricot sweets, and green to create a pistachio tart. You can use wax crayons or liquid colors depending on the desired effect. Place them in waxed paper holders for an even more realistic effect.

Another Idea

Color the clear gel wax depending on your preferred flavor of tea. For example, if you like mint, color the wax green and add mint-scented oil, then garnish with a mint tea bag and dried lemon slice. For hibiscus tea, color the wax red and garnish with cloves.

To Make the Candles

Materials

- Glass tea cup
- Tea bag
- 7 oz clear gel wax
- Orange coloring
- 2 white waxed wicks
- Honey-scented oil
- Dried orange slice
- Beeswax sheet
- Yellow and brown wax sheets

Equipment

- Double boiler
- Cotton cloth
- Cotton ball
- Rubbing alcohol
- Spoon
- Craft knife
- Needle

HINT

To blend the wafer's colors together and create a more realistic look, hold a heated knife blade along the edges to melt the wax.

1 Wash the inside of the glass cup using warm water and a damp cloth, then wipe the outside with a cotton ball dipped in rubbing alcohol. Insert a tea bag, making sure the tag hangs outside the cup.

2 Break the gel wax into small cubes and place them in a small pot. Add a few drops of honey-scented oil and orange coloring, then melt the wax in a double boiler over low heat, stirring constantly.

3 Slowly pour the wax into the clean glass without disturbing the tea bag. Let cool until it is semisolid.

4 Before the wax is completely solid, add the dried orange slice to the top. Make a hole with a needle through the center of the orange to the bottom of the glass and insert the waxed wick. Trim the wick to the desired height. Let the wax harden completely.

5 For the wafers, use a knife to cut a few strips of beeswax approximately 2½ × 1 inches.

6 Cut identical strips of wax from the brown and yellow sheets. Layer the three kinds of wax, alternating colors. Pierce a small hole at each end of the wafer and insert a short wick in each.

Frozen Treat Candle

These candles, inspired by 1950s ice cream parlors, are made with a variety of colorful waxes. Thanks to the strawberry and chocolate-scented oils, these candles give off a sweet and intense fragrance. The ice cream is decorated with details like a plastic spoon and a beeswax biscotti cookie.

An Alternative

For those who love the rich aroma of coffee, create a cafe-au-lait-inspired candle. Pour caramel-colored wax blended with coffee-scented oil in a mug and insert a wick. For a realistic effect, add a dollop of white wax "cream." To present the candle as a gift, wrap it in florist's paper with a few coffee beans scattered inside. Wrap the cup in the paper, tie with a raffia ribbon, and add a small sack of coffee beans.

To Make the Candles

Materials

- 10 ½ oz white wax
- Red and brown wax crayons
- Yellow liquid coloring
- Waxed wicks
- Chocolate and vanilla-scented oils
- Paper doilies
- Cocoa powder
- Sugar

Equipment

- Double boiler
- Craft knife
- Tea-light candle molds
- Flat dish
- Needle
- Fork
- Small pie tin

HINT

To easily remove the candle from the pie tin, add a few drops of oil to the tin and swab it with a cotton ball before pouring the wax. After the wax has hardened, you will have no trouble removing the candle.

1 Melt the white wax in a double boiler over low heat, then separate it into six roughly equal parts. Color the first part with a red wax crayon, another two with brown, and a third part yellow. Leave the last two parts white. Add 3 or 4 drops of vanilla-scented oil to the yellow and white waxes. Use chocolate-scented oil for the red and brown waxes.

2 Pour ⅛ inch of brown wax into a flat dish and allow it to cool, and then add a layer of white wax, again allowing it to cool completely. For the third layer, use beige wax, made by mixing the brown and white waxes. When this layer is partially solid, score the surface where you want to cut the slices, and pierce each slice's center with a needle. Insert wicks. When the wax is solid, remove the "cake" from the plate and cut into slices.

3 Make the petit fours using the brown and beige waxes, layering them in tea-light candle molds. Before the wax hardens, pierce the centers with a needle and insert the wicks. Remove the candles from the molds after they have hardened.

4 To make the tart, pour a thin layer of yellow wax into a small pie tin until it is just below the top. Let it cool, then add another thin layer of red wax on top of the yellow. Insert a wick and remove from the mold when hardened.

5 Heat the white wax in a double boiler. Before it has completely melted, mash it with a fork to create a foamy texture. Add dollops of white wax to each of the desserts. Sprinkle with real cocoa powder and sugar to garnish.

Chestnut Heart Candle

Your home will be ready for autumn with these tiny aromatic candles colored with chestnut tones. Their chocolate scent is fun and appetizing—just be sure your guests don't mistake them for candy!

As Gifts

Here is a simple but charming way to present these unique tea lights. Fill a wicker basket with fresh moss and arrange the chestnut hearts on top. Add a few small acorns or pinecones to continue the autumn theme.

How, When, Where

These candles make a beautiful centerpiece for an autumn dinner party. Fill a wide, clear bowl with water and float five of the chestnut heart candles on the water. Add a few red and yellow fabric leaves to drift among the candles.

To Make the Candles

Materials

- White wax, 1 oz per candle
- Dark brown liquid coloring
- Waxed wicks
- Chocolate-scented oil
- Light brown liquid wax pen

Equipment

- Double boiler
- Plastic heart molds
- Needle
- Scissors
- Flat paintbrush
- Matches

1 Melt the white wax in a double boiler over low heat, then add 5 drops of brown coloring and 3 drops of chocolate-scented oil.

2 Pour the wax into plastic heart molds and let cool.

3 When the wax is completely solid, remove the candles by applying light pressure to the molds.

HINT

To fix a smeared paint job, wait until the top half of the candle is dry. Put a few drops of liquid wax onto a piece of plastic wrap and dip the paintbrush into the wax. Carefully paint over the smeared portion, repeating if necessary after it dries.

4 With a light brown liquid wax pen, add a few drops of wax to the top half of each heart. Use a flat paintbrush to spread the wax with long, smooth strokes. Let dry.

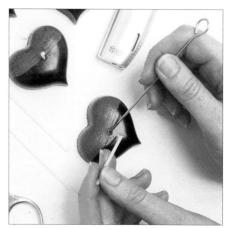

5 Heat the tip of a needle with a match, then pierce the candle through its center and insert the waxed wick. Trim to desired height.

Cannoli Candle

Why not warm up a friendly gathering with these unique candles shaped like cannolis? These delectable desserts are made with colorful yellow wax and decorated with cream and candy sprinkles, also made of wax. Burning slowly, these candles release a warm and sweet vanilla scent.

As Gifts

Place six cannoli candles on a doily and wrap in a pastry box as if they came straight from the bakery. What a surprise to find these sweet candles inside. Doilies can also be used in your home as candleholders. For an extra touch, add a few drops of vanilla-scented oil to the paper.

Another Idea

Create a variety of tiny dessert candles. To create layered pastries, for example, use several small squares of beeswax. Between each square, add a dollop of white wax "cream" and continue the layers until you reach the desired height. Use this same technique to make cookie candles and other treats.

To Make the Candles

Materials

- 1 ¾ oz wax flakes
- Vanilla-scented oil
- Waxed wicks
- Thin cardboard
- Aluminum foil
- Plastic film canister or other holder
- Red, green, yellow, and brown wax
- Yellow coloring

Equipment

- Double boiler
- Fork
- Scissors
- Knife
- Heat-resistant adhesive tape
- Needle

1 Take two-thirds of the wax and add 5 drops of vanilla-scented oil and 4 drops of yellow coloring, then melt in a double boiler over low heat.

2 Make a rolled-up cardboard tube that's about 2½ inches long and hold it closed with heat-resistant adhesive tape. Cover the inside and one end with a strip of aluminum foil, then insert the tube partially into a plastic film canister or other suitable holder.

3 Pour the yellow wax into the tube, filling it until it is about ½ inch from the top. Let partially solidify, then remove the candle from the mold.

HINT

Another way to make the cannoli body, instead of using melted wax, is to use beeswax sheets. Cut a strip from the beeswax about 3½ × 2½ inches, then roll it in the same way as if you were making a real cannoli.

4 Melt the remaining wax, adding a few drops of vanilla-scented oil and 1 drop of yellow coloring. Let the wax cool slightly and mash it with a fork to create a creamy texture.

5 Using the fork, add "cream" to each end of the cannoli, pressing lightly to attach. Let cool completely.

6 Use a needle to pierce the center of the cannoli and insert the waxed wick. Decorate with candy sprinkles made from bits of red, green, yellow, and brown wax rolled into tiny balls.

Ladybug Candle

Ladybugs are thought to bring happiness and fortune wherever they alight—why not light your house with several of these red and black candles to bring good luck? The strawberry-scented wax provides a sweet way to add fragrance to your children's playroom, even if the candles aren't lit.

As Gifts

Aladybug candle makes a novel and delightful gift. Place the ladybug on a large fabric leaf and wrap it in a piece of transparent cellophane. Tie the package with a thin red ribbon, knotting a twig with fabric leaves in the bow.

How, When, Where

Why not use these simple, fun ladybugs as place-holders for your child's birthday party? Place each ladybug on a leaf of green construction paper with a guest's name on it. Float two or three ladybugs in a bowl of water as a centerpiece.

To Make the Candles

Materials

- White wax granules, 2 ½ oz per candle
- Black coloring
- Red and black wax sheets
- Waxed wicks
- Strawberry-scented oil

Equipment

- Double boiler
- Round mold
- Scissors

1 Melt the white wax granules in a double boiler over low heat. Add a few drops of black coloring and 5 drops of strawberry-scented oil.

2 Pour the melted black wax into a round mold, forming a layer about 1 to 1 ½ inches high. Let cool until the wax has partially hardened.

3 Before the wax solidifies, insert a measured waxed wick. Allow to cool completely, then remove the candle from the mold.

HINT

To attach the small circles and antennae to the ladybug, heat them slightly between your hands and affix them by applying light pressure with your fingers. To complete the project, heat the finished candle with a hair dryer held at least 8 inches away.

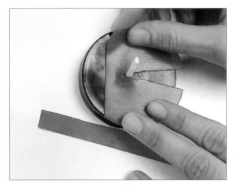

4 From the red wax sheet, cut a circle slightly larger than the diameter of the black candle. Remove a section from the edge about ½ inch wide and, on the opposite side, cut out a triangular wedge, the point of which will be about ½ inch from the first cut. Place the red "wings" on the body, fitting the point of the triangle around the wick, and folding the sides down over the candle.

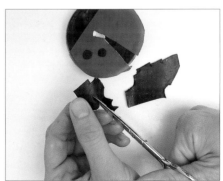

5 From the black wax sheet, cut a few small circles and 2-inch-long strips to use as antennae. Place these wax decorations on the ladybug by applying light pressure with your fingers. Once attached, curl the ends of the antennae slightly.

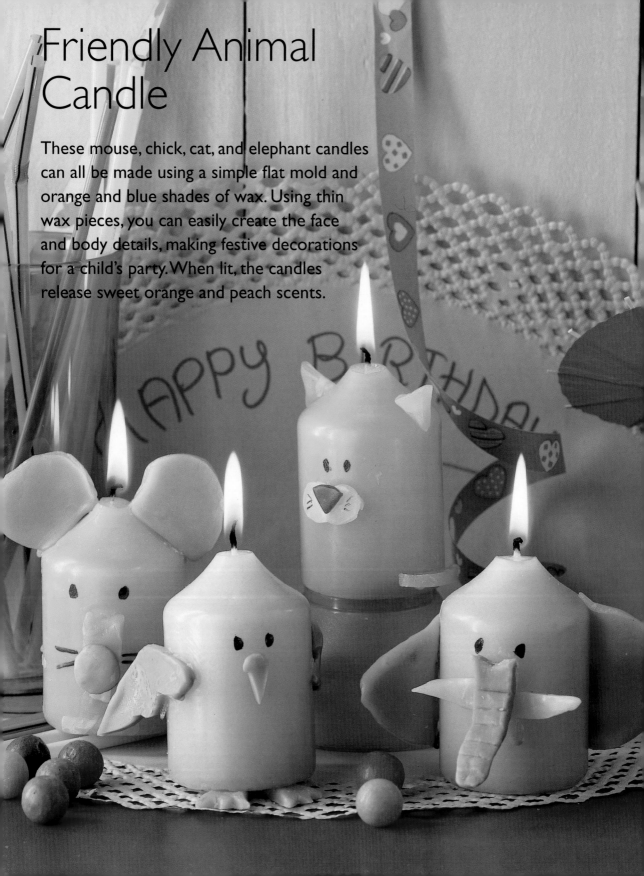

Friendly Animal Candle

These mouse, chick, cat, and elephant candles can all be made using a simple flat mold and orange and blue shades of wax. Using thin wax pieces, you can easily create the face and body details, making festive decorations for a child's party. When lit, the candles release sweet orange and peach scents.

An Alternative

Use shades of pastel blue, white, and yellow to create this daisy candle scented with chamomile. Create thin films of white and yellow wax and carve out petals and flower centers from the wax. Attach the petals to a pastel blue cylindrical candle for a simple way to enhance any room.

How, When, Where

You can use essential oils to help your child relax at the end of a long day. For an energetic child, scent the candle with chamomile and diffuse a bowl of water scented with one drop each of chamomile, lavender, and lemon into the air. If your child has a stomachache, add dill-scented oil to either the candle or the water.

To Make the Candles

Materials
- 1 ¾ oz white wax granules
- Orange, blue, and red coloring
- 2 orange and 2 pastel blue cylindrical candles
- Orange and peach-scented oils

Equipment
- Double boiler
- Spoon
- Shallow tin mold
- Lighter
- Black felt-tipped marker
- Knife

1 Melt the wax granules in a double boiler over low heat, stirring constantly. Add 5 drops of orange-scented oil and a few drops of orange coloring.

2 Pour the melted wax into a shallow tin, creating a thin layer of wax. Allow to cool completely.

3 With a knife, carve out the ears and tail for the cat. Make separate layers of red and white waxes from which to cut the nose and mouth.

HINT

Create a blue chick with a yellow beak and feet. For the elephant, make a blue trunk and ears and white tusks. For the mouse, make orange ears and a blue nose.

4 Use a lighter to slightly heat the edge of the wax ears and tails. Attach by applying light pressure with your fingertips. Add the mouth and nose in the same way.

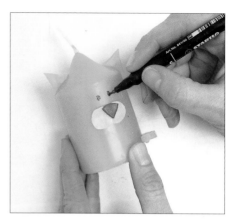

5 Draw the eyes and whiskers of the cat on the candle using a black felt-tipped marker. Follow the same process to create an orange mouse and a blue peach-scented chick and elephant.

71

Ghost Candle

On Halloween, legend has it that witches, ghosts, and spirits walk the earth. Decorate for the season and amuse your children by creating these tiny white ghost candles. White wax is poured into little molds; the resulting candles are decorated with white wings and black eyes. Honey-scented oil, with its sweet and relaxing fragrance, will help calm your children after a busy night of trick-or-treating.

As Gifts

Wrap two or three ghost candles in a lightly crumpled sheet of orange tissue paper. Loosely wrap the candles in the paper, allowing the paper to billow out in a rounded shape. Tie with a piece of natural cord. Draw a triangular nose and eyes and a mischievous grin to resemble a jack-o'-lantern.

An Alternative

Color the wax in several different shades to make unique place-holders for a Halloween party. Attach a square of white rice paper under each candle and write the name of each guest with ink the same shade as the candle.

To Make the Candles

Materials
- Opaque white wax, 1 oz per candle
- Waxed wicks
- Honey-scented oil
- Black liquid wax pen

Equipment
- Double boiler
- Small domed mold
- Needle
- Modeling clay
- Scissors
- Wax paper
- Craft knife

1 Pierce the top of a small domed mold with a needle.

2 Insert a waxed wick through the hole and fix it in place with a piece of modeling clay to avoid wax leakage. Melt the wax in a double boiler over low heat and add 3 drops of honey-scented oil.

3 Prop the mold between two jar lids so the wick isn't pressed against the table, then fill it almost to the top with the melted wax. Allow it to cool completely and remove the candle.

HINT

Another way to make the wings is to pour a ½-inch-thick layer of wax into an aluminum tray. Remove the wax layer, then cut out the wings and attach them by melting their edges on the bottom of a warm pot for a few seconds.

4 Carefully pour a ½-inch-thick layer of wax onto a sheet of wax paper. Let cool. Use a knife to cut out two small wings for each ghost. Attach with a little melted wax.

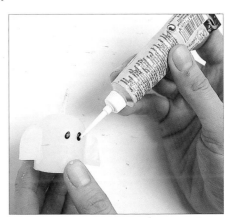

5 Trim the wick, then add two small eyes using a black liquid wax pen. Let dry for several hours.

Flower Bouquet Candle

This cheerful bouquet is made by
using brightly colored wax to
create miniature tulips: The petals
and leaves are made from wax
sheets and attached to a tall,
green tapered candle.
Place the tulips in a
clear vase filled with
sand for a unique center-
piece. Ylang-ylang oil,
rubbed on the flowers,
releases a smooth, refreshing
scent.

An Alternative

Make brightly colored taper centerpieces to brighten your next garden party. Cut a long thin strip from a sheet of red wax and spiral it around a green taper. Complete the candle by adding a few small strips of green wax, attached at the tip of the taper, slightly below the wick.

Special Scents

These candles are a fast and simple way to scent a room. Many store-bought candles are made with synthetic scents, which create an artificial fragrance that can be unpleasant or overpowering. It's usually better to buy unscented candles and add your own scented oil. To do this, put 8 to 10 drops of oil on a cotton ball and rub it on the candle's surface to disperse the fragrance.

To Make the Candles

Materials
- Red, blue, pink, yellow, and green wax sheets
- Bright green tapered candles
- Ylang-ylang oil

Equipment
- Pen or pencil
- Craft knife
- Cotton ball
- Drawing paper

Pattern for petal

HINT

When you shape the petals on the taper, be sure the wax is warm to prevent them from falling off. If the petals or the leaves fall off the taper, the wax is too cold. Slightly warm the wax in your hand or with a match, then reattach to the candle.

1 Using the pattern, draw five petals on a piece of paper. Place the paper on the red wax sheet and use a knife to cut out each petal. Apply light pressure to the back of the wax sheet to carefully remove each petal.

2 Add a few drops of ylang-ylang oil to a cotton ball and rub it over the entire length of a taper. Let it dry completely.

3 Use your fingers to attach the petals to the taper, with each of their bases about 1½ inches below the wick. Slightly overlap the bases and shape the petals so they curve outward.

4 Cut a leaf from a green wax sheet and score veins on it with a knife, being careful not to cut completely through.

5 With a light pressure, attach the leaf to the candle at the desired height. Repeat these steps to create blue, pink, and yellow tulips.

Autumn Leaf Candle

In autumn, leaves fall . . . onto ivory wax, creating lovely candles
with luminous colors. The opaque wax, holding the autumn leaves,
is scented with white musk oil. It
releases a delicate scent,
creating a relaxing,
balanced atmosphere.

As Gifts

Decorate the candle package in an autumn theme: Twist a few cords of orange, red, and brown raffia ribbons together, then tear a square from a piece of handmade paper and glue a colorful leaf in its center. Tie the raffia ribbon and tag around the candle.

How, When, Where

You can use autumn leaves to create a variety of interesting patterns. Arrange the leaves by slightly overlapping them or by spreading several small leaves around the candle. You can also use this method to cover the candle with pressed dried flowers for a completely different look.

To Make the Candle

Materials

- Large ivory pillar candle
- 1 ¾ oz opaque white wax
- Musk-scented oil
- Dried autumn leaves

Equipment

- Double boiler
- Wooden spoon

1 Melt the opaque white wax in a double boiler over low heat and add 10 drops of musk-scented oil.

2 Gently dip the leaves, one at a time, into the melted wax. Attach the leaves to the pillar candle's surface, smoothing them with your hands.

HINT

Before attaching the leaves to the candle, lightly rub the candle's surface with a cotton ball dipped in rubbing alcohol, then let it dry. To avoid burning yourself, use a pair of tweezers to dip the leaves into the melted wax.

3 Slightly overlap all the leaves until you achieve the desired look.

4 When the wax layer over the leaves has hardened, carefully dip the entire candle into the still-melted wax, holding it by the wick. Let it cool completely.

Floating Candle

A colorful and aromatic way to welcome spring—
tea-light candles that release an intense jasmine
fragrance, full of energizing properties. Float the tea
lights in a bowl of water with fresh flowers drifting
among the candles. It's a simple and beautiful
centerpiece that imitates
the sweet scent of
the season.

An Alternative

Decorate the floating candles by drawing simple flower outlines on their surfaces with a silver liquid wax pen. Let the wax dry for about 12 hours, then place each tea light in an individual glass of water and use them as place-holders.

As Gifts

Create scented favors to give your guests at Easter: Wrap each tea light in a sheet of pastel tissue paper to match the color of the wax, then add curled ribbons so the packages resemble little Easter eggs.

To Make the Candles

Materials

- Jar lids approximately 2 inches wide
- 17 oz wax flakes
- Waxed wicks
- Jasmine-scented oil
- Light green, pink, yellow and purple wax crayons

Equipment

- Double boiler
- Spoon
- Scissors
- Needle

1 Melt 4 ½ ounces of wax in a double boiler over low heat, stirring often. Crumble a small piece of pink crayon into the wax and allow it to melt completely. The wax should be a consistent color and free of lumps.

2 Add 5 drops of jasmine-scented oil to the wax and stir carefully. If you want a stronger scent, add more oil (10 or so drops is probably too much, however).

3 Slowly pour the wax into a jar lid, making sure that it doesn't leak over the edge. If this happens, quickly clean it with a cloth before the wax hardens. Let cool approximately 15 minutes.

HINT

Before pouring the wax in the lids, clean them thoroughly with hot water and dry them with a paper towel. To make it easy to remove the candles from the molds, grease the lids with a few drops of oil on a cotton ball, swabbing the insides before adding the wax. Or you can put the molds in the freezer for a few minutes after the wax has cooled.

4 When the wax is partially solid and has formed a patina, pierce a hole through its center with a needle. Gently insert a waxed wick about ½ inch high. Allow the wax to harden completely.

5 Remove the candle from the mold by turning it upside down and applying light pressure. Repeat the process to make candles in a variety of colors.

Floating Heart Candle

Impress friends with this beautiful centerpiece made of floating heart candles and red sand. The candlelight is reflected upon the water's surface— a beautiful effect—while the sweet rose scent is gently released.

An Alternative

For a formal dinner party or to grace a buffet table, decorate the bases of short, clear glasses with elegant red ribbon. Fill the glasses with water and place a floating heart in each one. Or, for a place-holder, attach the candle to a red construction paper heart, cut slightly larger than the candle.

To Make the Candles

Materials

- Rose-scented red heart tea lights (if you can't find scented tea lights, add a few drops of rose-scented oil to a cotton ball and swab unscented candles).
- Sheet of red corrugated cardboard
- Modeling clay
- Green thread or ribbon
- Mixed green and yellow sand
- Red sand
- 3 long wooden sticks
- 3 colorful cups
- Glass saucer and bowl

Equipment

- Scissors
- Pen or pencil
- Sheet of drawing paper
- Skewer or needle

Pattern for flowers

1 Use the pattern to draw a flower outline on paper and three flowers on the back of a piece of red corrugated cardboard. Cut out the flowers.

2 Mold three small balls of modeling clay with your hands, making each about the size of a grape, then place each on the tip of a wooden stick. Shape with your fingers to flatten the tops.

3 Use a skewer to pierce a hole in the centers of the cardboard flowers. Place a candle over the center of the flower, corrugated side up, and pierce a hole through the cardboard and bottom of the candle with the skewer, or with a sharp needle or nail.

4 Place the heart and flower on the clay, then push the stick through the clay and into the previously made hole. Use your fingers to fasten the clay to the cardboard. Wrap green thread or ribbon around the clay to conceal it.

5 Pour green and yellow sand in a cup until it's about 2 inches from the top. Insert the wooden candlestick into the cup, embedding it in the sand. Make two more "plants" using the same method.

6 Complete the arrangement by adding red sand to a glass bowl until it's about 2 inches from the top. Cover with an inch of water, and add a few floating hearts to the surface, making sure not to wet the wicks.

Blue Glass Floating Candle

Create a small mountain lake for the middle of your living room. This centerpiece, embossed with blue patterns and filled with water, will transport you to a relaxing retreat as you gaze at the deep blue floating candles drifting inside the clear glass bowl.

An Alternative

Another way to use sea glass and floating candles is by making individual place-holders. All you need are a few small round drinking glasses, transparent gel wax, and waxed wicks. Carefully remove the original wick from the floating candle and insert one suitable to the height of the glass. Place a blue glass pebble at the bottom of the drinking glass and pour in about 1 inch of gel wax (after melting it in a double boiler). Let the wax solidify, then place the floating candle and wick on top of the first layer. Cover it with more gel wax until you reach the top of the glass, being careful not to cover the wick. Let it cool completely before lighting the candle.

To Make the Candle

Materials
- 3 blue floating candles
- 15 blue glass pebbles
- Blue paint for glass
- Clear glass bowl
- Glue

Equipment
- Rubbing alcohol
- Cotton cloth

HINT
You might want to add a layer of blue sand to the bottom of the bowl before placing the pebbles. Pour the sand about ½ inch high on the bottom of the bowl, position the glass pebbles, and fill with water. If the pebbles move while you're pouring the water, reposition them before adding the candles.

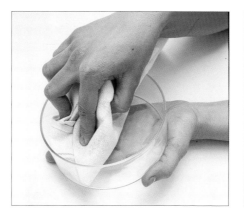

1 Carefully clean the glass bowl using a cotton cloth soaked with rubbing alcohol. This will ensure that the paint and glue stick to the glass.

2 Glue eight blue glass pebbles to the outside of the bowl, positioning four on opposite sides of the bowl about ½ inch from the upper edge. Glue the next four pebbles in between the first ones but placed lower on the bowl.

3 Before you paint the bowl, make a few practice patterns of dots and stripes on a piece of paper until you determine the pattern you like best. Then decorate the bowl around the blue glass pebbles.

4 Let the bowl dry for at least 6 hours. Arrange seven blue glass pebbles on the bottom of the bowl and fill three-fourths full with water. Carefully lay three floating candles on the surface, making sure not to wet the wicks.

Floating Leaf Candle

A wooden twig keeps these leaves floating together in a bowl with fresh flowers. This delicate springtime centerpiece is reminiscent of a Japanese garden. The musk oil released from the candles penetrates the room with its relaxing scent.

As Gifts

Make a giant yellow candy wrapper to enclose the floating leaves. Take a sheet of yellow tissue paper, crumple it slightly with your fingers, then wrap the candles in a row. Tie the ends with a couple loops of leafy green wire.

How, When, Where

Create individual place-holders by filling small glass cups with yellow-colored water and placing a floating leaf on the surface. If you like, add a fresh flower. Decorate the table in shades of green and yellow as a final touch.

To Make the Candle

Materials

- 3 floating green leaf candles scented with musk (if you can't find scented leaf candles, add a few drops of oil to a cotton ball and swab unscented ones)
- 2 skewers
- Wooden twig
- Green raffia ribbon
- Fresh flowers
- Glass bowl

Equipment

- Straight-tipped cuticle scissors

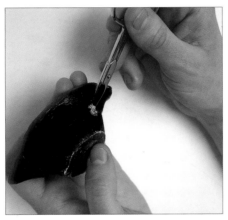

1 With the tip of the scissors, puncture a hole about 1 to 1½ inches deep about 1 inch from the base of the leaf candle. Be careful not to break or otherwise ruin the wax.

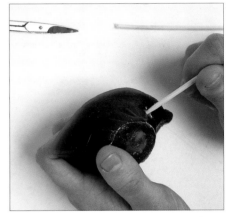

2 Take two skewers and cut them into three or four parts, each about 1½ to 2 inches long; discard the pointed tips. Insert a skewer segment into the hole of the leaf, sinking it deeply into the wax.

HINT

Before completing the centerpiece, make sure all the leaves are straight and secure on the branch. If the arrangement is unbalanced when it's floating, one of the leaves could dip underwater, wetting the wick.

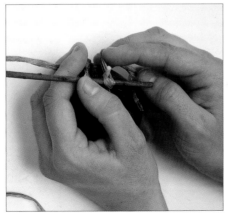

3 Tie the leaf to the wooden branch by wrapping a piece of green raffia ribbon around one end of the twig and then knotting the ribbon to the stick inserted in the candle.

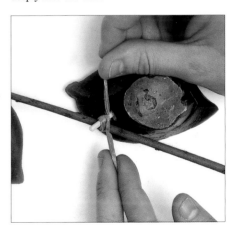

4 Repeat the process, tying the other two leaves about 3 or 4 inches apart from each other. Fill a small bowl with water and add the floating branch and leaves. Add some fresh flowers for an elegant touch.

Pastel Straw Candle

Make an unusual candle using drinking straws in translucent pastel shades. The wax wraps around the straws, creating a veiled effect, while the sweet and intense vanilla essence makes it perfect for an evening of relaxation.

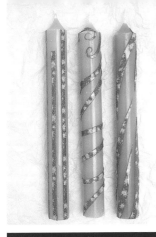

An Alternative

Update all sorts of candles around the house by decorating them with printed wax sheets. Tapered candles, for example, can be decorated by wrapping thin ribbons of the printed wax around the candle, as if they are climbing vines. For a final touch, decorate the candleholder with fabric ivy.

How, When, Where

To attain your desired scent, use scented candles or swab unscented candles with your chosen fragrance. Once you light the candles, the heat will quickly diffuse the scent throughout the room. Remember to never use oils that contain alcohol because they are flammable.

To Make the Candle

Materials

- Tall white candle with a squared base
- Printed green wax sheets
- Green wax thread
- Eucalyptus-scented oil
- Thin cardboard

Equipment

- Cotton ball
- Scissors
- Craft knife
- Pen or pencil

1 Moisten a cotton ball with a few drops of eucalyptus-scented oil and wipe it over the entire surface of the candle. Let dry for a few minutes.

2 Draw your leaves of grass on a sheet of thin cardboard and then cut out the shapes.

3 Place the cutouts on the back of a printed wax sheet. Trace the outlines with a pen, then use a knife to cut out the shapes.

HINT

After decorating the candle, heat it with a hair dryer. The wax sheets and thread will then be malleable, and you will be able to touch up any problems and securely fasten the wax to the candle.

4 Warm the wax cutouts by holding them in your hands for a few moments. Carefully remove the protective film from the wax and attach each blade to the candle, applying light pressure with your fingers.

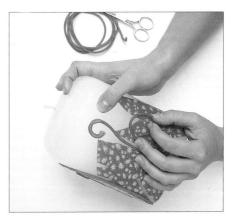

5 Cut a few different lengths from the green wax thread and fasten them to the candle by applying light pressure. Curl the tips.

Bamboo Candle

Just visible within this white candle are various heights of bamboo, which add a distinctive touch to the piece and create a luminous effect. Perfect to light when curled up with your favorite book, the candle releases a delicate musk scent that inspires a meditative atmosphere.

As Gifts

Present the bamboo candle wrapped in shades of bright yellow and pale green. Wrap the candle in a sheet of slightly crumpled yellow tissue and tie the ends with a green organza ribbon knotted in a bow. Glue a few bamboo rods on the outside of the package and tie some in the ribbon to give this unique candle a natural feel.

Another Idea

Vary the placement of the bamboo pieces within the candle to create different visual effects. For example, pour a thin layer of wax in the mold and lay a few rods lengthwise across the bottom. Cover with another layer of wax and continue layering rods and wax until you reach the top. Then, when the candle is lit, you will see the ends of the bamboo illuminated through the wax instead of the sides.

To Make the Candle

Materials

- 10 ½ oz white wax
- Waxed wick
- Musk-scented oil
- Milk carton
- Bamboo rods

Equipment

- Double boiler
- Craft knife
- Needle
- Scissors

1 Melt the wax in a double boiler over low heat and add 6 drops of musk-scented oil.

2 With the knife, cut the end off a milk carton to create a square mold. Cut the bamboo rods into various lengths no longer than the height of the mold. Dip each rod into the melted wax and fasten it onto the inside of the carton, covering all four sides with bamboo.

HINT

Be careful when dipping the bamboo into the melted wax; to avoid burning yourself, you might want to use tweezers. When placing the pieces in the mold, work quickly so the wax doesn't harden before you have a chance to position the bamboo the way you want it.

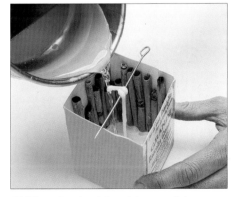

3 Wrap the tip of the wick around the needle and support it on the rim of the carton so the wick remains in the center. Pour melted wax into the mold until you reach the top.

4 When the wax has completely hardened, unwrap the wick from the needle and cut it to the desired height. Remove the candle from the mold, carefully tearing off the carton if necessary.

French Provincial Candle

Create a touch of provincial France in your home by decorating candles of various shapes and heights with imaginatively patterned wax sheets. Easy to apply, these wax sheets will fasten to any type of candle simply by heating. The lily scent releases a sweet, embracing fragrance.

An Alternative

Try alternating printed wax sheets with solid colors. A square-based candle can be covered on each side with differently colored wax sheets, then enhanced by wrapping a strip of printed wax vertically over the candle and covering the top with another square of printed wax.

How, When, Where

If you'd like to put these provincial candles in your bedroom, scent them with relaxing jasmine, rose, ylang-ylang, or bergamot. Use lavender to help induce sleep.

To Make the Candles

Materials

- Cylindrical candles
- Printed wax sheets with provincial designs
- Lily-scented oil

Equipment

- Cotton ball
- Nail scissors

1 Moisten a cotton ball with a few drops of lily-scented oil and swab the candle over its entire surface. Let dry.

2 Heat the wax sheet by gently pressing it between your hands, then carefully separate the wax from its protective film.

3 Wrap the wax sheet around the candle, leaving extra wax at the top and base. Press to secure the wax.

HINT

The wax sheets will mold perfectly to the candle if they are heated in your hands before attaching. You should also wrap your hands around the candle after attaching the wax sheets so the heat will help the candle and the wax meld. If you try to separate the wax sheet from its protective film and it does not easily come apart, carefully warm it with a match.

4 Cut several slits in the printed wax at the top and base of the candle. This will allow you to fold the wax down onto the top and bottom of the candle.

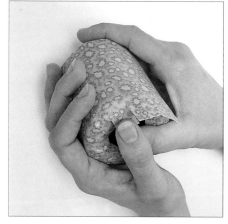

5 Press the wax down at the base of the candle, overlapping the wax slightly at the slits so it lies flat. Do the same at the top of the candle, leaving the area around the wick open.

Toile Candle

The French elegance of woven toile is featured on this decorative candle. The wax used to fasten the toile to the candle is scented with vanilla, releasing a warm and relaxing scent as it melts.

As Gifts

Make a simple package that offers a glimpse of the colorful candle. Wrap the candle in a square of cellophane, gathering it at the top. Tie the package with a large bow the same color as the felt. To create a holiday look, spray the package with glitter.

How, When, Where

These colorful candles can be used to brighten any room in your home, or to decorate your table at a friendly dinner. Use various colors and designs, or cut out the name of each guest to create place-holders.

To Make the Candle

Materials
- Small glass vase
- 7 oz opaque white wax
- Waxed wick with metal base
- Sheet of red felt, 4 × 12 inches
- Glitter spray
- Cinnamon-scented oil

Equipment
- Double boiler
- Skewer
- Scissors
- Spray adhesive

1 Support the wick in the center of the vase by wrapping one end around a skewer and balancing the stick on the rim of the vase so the wick remains vertical.

2 Melt the wax in a double boiler over low heat and add 5 drops of cinnamon-scented oil.

3 Pour the melted wax into the vase until it's about ½ inch from the top, being careful not to move the wick. Let cool completely.

HINT

Before cutting designs out of the felt, first make a stencil from a piece of cardboard. Place the stencil on the felt and outline the shapes with a white colored pencil, then cut out the patterns.

4 Measure and cut out a rectangle of felt that will fit the height and circumference of the vase. Use scissors to cut petal and leaf designs in the felt.

5 Spray the back of the felt with adhesive, holding the can at least 12 inches from the surface. Fasten the felt to the vase, making sure its edges join together along the side.

6 Spray the vase with glitter to create a sparkling effect.

107

Perfumed Paper and Leaf Candle

The decoupage technique is used to create these beautiful tea-light holders decorated with natural paper and small leaves. When the candles are lit, the light will shine through the paper, adding a decorative touch to any table.

An Alternative

Design an elegant rosy place-holder by covering a glass candleholder with rice paper printed with small flowers. Perfume the wax with geranium-scented oil, which has a delicate scent similar to that of rose.

How, When, Where

If you have a patio, you can create a stunning center-piece for your first spring dinner. Use a high cylindrical glass vase to shield the flame from the wind. Cover it with rice paper of any color you choose, then decoupage it with small dried flowers. Insert a colored candle that matches the rice paper as a finishing touch.

To Make the Candle

Materials
- Fuchsia rice paper
- Small dried and pressed leaves
- 3 ½ oz opaque wax
- Rose-scented oil
- Green coloring
- Tea-light mold
- Waxed wick
- Glass candleholder
- Decoupage glue

Equipment
- Double boiler
- Bowl
- Small paintbrush
- Scissors
- Ruler

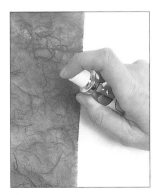

1 Measure and cut a piece of rice paper to cover the glass candleholder. Spritz the paper with rose-scented oil and let dry.

2 Dilute the glue with water according to the glue's instructions. Spread a thin layer on the back of the paper and attach it to the glass. Let it dry completely. Use the same method to attach the leaves to the paper, then paint over the leaves with the decoupage glue.

3 Melt the wax in a double boiler over low heat and color it with 4 drops of green coloring. Add 8 drops of rose-scented oil.

HINT

The usual ratio for decoupage glue is three parts water and one part glue. To attach the pressed leaves on the paper more securely, use a slightly denser solution made of two parts water and one part glue.

4 Pour the wax into the tea-light mold until you reach the top. Let it cool until par-tially solid.

5 When the wax is partially solid, insert a wick and cut it to the desired height. Let the candle harden completely, then place it into the decorated glass.

Scented Lantern

Create these elegant embroidered lanterns by making a rigid structure of wooden dowels and placing a tea light in the center. The weave of the material allows light to shine through and create intricate patterns. Lemongrass oil perfumes the wax with its mossy fragrance, creating a comfortable, natural atmosphere.

As Gifts

Fold up the woven candleholder and attach a small matching votive, tying the package with a ribbon in a contrasting color. To complete the gift, include a bottle of the essential oil you used to scent the candle.

How, When, Where

Vary the color and texture of the material you use for the lantern to match the décor of the room you want to fragrance. For the kitchen, use woven tartan and scent the candle with lemon, verbena, or orange. For a child's playroom, use colorful printed material and a candle scented with chamomile or vanilla oil. For your bedroom, scent the candle with rose, lavender, or geranium.

To Make the Lantern

Materials

- Woven green linen, approximately 12 × 20 inches and stiff enough to stand upright
- Round ivory doily
- 8 wooden dowels, ¼-inch diameter, each about 4 inches long
- Small green candle
- Lemongrass-scented oil

Equipment

- Sewing needle
- Thread
- Scissors
- Cotton ball

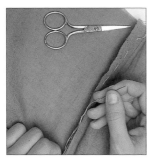

1 Cut four rectangles from a square of green linen, each about 11½ × 4½ inches. Sew them together in a row along their long edges, keeping the good side of the material on the outside.

2 Fold over the top edge of the rectangle and sew along the edge, leaving a sleeve about 1 inch wide so you can insert a dowel. Repeat with the bottom edge. Sew the two short edges of the rectangle together to close the lantern, leaving space at the top and bottom edges to insert the dowels. Do not seal the opening.

3 Fold the front face of the linen in the center and cut out a circular shape slightly smaller than the doily. Place the doily on the outside of the lantern, covering the hole, and sew around its edge from the inside using small stitches.

HINT

When attaching the doily to the lantern, make the seam on the back of the linen using thin thread. Insert the needle through the center of the doily's edge, then pass it back through the linen. Do not pull on the stitches.

4 Insert four dowels in both the top and bottom of the lantern.

5 Moisten a cotton ball with a few drops of lemongrass-scented oil and rub it over the entire surface of the candle. Position the candle inside the lantern in the center. Make a similar candleholder using the same method, but use ivory eyelet material instead of linen.

Threaded Wax Egg Candle

These egg-shaped candles are covered with wax threads in warm shades of red and yellow. Unique in appearance and fragrance, the eggs are rubbed with clover-scented oil, which releases a slow, sweet fragrance perfect for your kitchen.

An Alternative

Use bright colors to make cheerful alternatives to one-toned candles; alternate between red, green, and blue wax threads to create a layered effect. Place the candles on wooden egg cups as modern candlesticks. Or carefully position the egg candles on a bed of fake moss or grass. Enhance the arrangement by adding a few fresh flowers.

How, When, Where

Set aside a few moments for relaxation. Immerse yourself in a warm bath perfumed with jasmine-scented oil and place these eggs on candleholders near the bathtub. Scent the candles with the same floral essence.

To Make the Candles

Materials

- 3 egg-shaped white candles
- Colorful wax thread
- Clover-scented oil
- Small straight pin

Equipment

- Cotton ball
- Cotton cloth
- Scissors

1 Wipe the egg candle with a clean cloth, then polish its surface using a cotton ball moistened with a few drops of clover-scented oil.

2 Unroll a string of colored wax thread and heat it with your fingers until it becomes soft and malleable.

HINT

If the wax thread stretches and detaches from the egg, it's probably because both are too cold. Wrap the egg in a warm cloth for several minutes to soften the wax without deforming it, then slowly wrap the wax string around the egg as you heat it with your fingers.

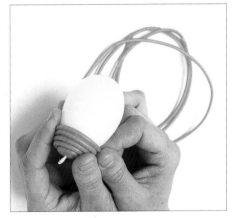

3 Starting near the wick, wrap the wax string around the egg, applying light pressure with your fingers to fasten it. Keep the turns very straight so you don't leave white space.

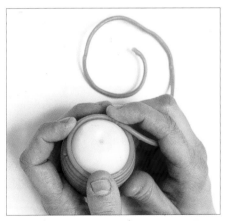

4 Cover the egg in this fashion, maintaining tight turns and molding the string to the egg's curved surface. To secure the tip of the thread to the bottom indentation of the egg, insert a small straight pin through the string into the base.

Confetti Candle

Create a cheerful environment with these
two-toned candles topped with wax
"confetti." Use blue and violet for the base
and a rose-colored shade for the top. The
unmelted wax flakes look like confetti
that fell from the sky. Rose-scented
oil releases its delicate fragrance,
perfuming the entire room.

An Alternative

Here's a quick way to decorate for a formal dinner: Fill a few glasses with orange sand and sprinkle some yellow wax flakes on top. Insert a wick, and the candles will light up the table in a simple and stylish fashion.

How, When, Where

Accompany this centerpiece with similar place-holders: Create wax bowl candles from small glass fingerbowls and float a tea light in the center of each. Use different shades to create a tonal effect.

To Make the Candle

Materials
- 7 oz white wax granules
- Varying shades of yellow wax flakes
- Floating tea lights
- Musk-scented oil

Equipment
- Double boiler
- Spoon
- 2 different-sized round glass bowls, one smaller than the other

1 Place the white wax flakes or granules in the small pot of a double boiler and melt them over low heat, stirring often. Add 5 drops of musk-scented oil and stir to disperse.

2 Pour the melted wax into a large glass bowl and tilt and rotate the bowl so the wax covers the bottom and sides completely. Let this layer cool, and then add another layer of the same wax to increase the thickness. Let this layer cool.

3 Scatter colored wax flakes in the waxed bowl so the bottom is completely covered.

HINT

Before you pour the melted white wax over the wax flakes, let it cool slightly so that it doesn't completely melt the inner portion. Leaving the flakes slightly intact adds a pleasing look to the project.

4 Pour the melted white wax on top of the colored flakes to the top of the mold and let cool for several minutes. Press a smaller glass bowl into the center of the still-soft wax and press it down to create a smooth indentation. Let cool, leaving the smaller bowl positioned in the center.

5 When the wax has completely hardened, remove the small bowl from the candle center; also remove the entire candle from the larger bowl. Fill the indentation with water, add a few drops of musk-scented oil, and float tea lights in the center.

Japanese Lantern Candle

Inspired by simple Japanese elegance, these candles are made with opaque wax tiles in delicate tones of blue and pink. The ivory candle contrasts serenely with the colored wax. It's held together with three simple strands of raffia. The lemongrass scent warms the room with a pleasant woodsy fragrance.

An Alternative

Instead of using cocktail glasses, you can arrange colorful wax powder in a glass bowl, making star or flower shapes with the sand. Use a wide decorative bowl and insert several wicks to create a bright and aromatic centerpiece.

Scenting the Candle

Lemongrass is not universally appreciated: Some people enjoy it, while others find it unbearable. Those who don't like the scent, however, can still appreciate its stress-relieving and stimulating properties. In Sri Lanka, this essence is known as the oil of tranquility.

To Make the Candles

Materials

- Lemongrass-scented oil
- Powder wax in many colors
- Semi-rigid wax wicks
- Cocktail glasses in various shapes

Equipment

- Small paintbrush
- Skewer
- Rubbing alcohol
- Cotton cloth

1 Carefully clean the glass with a cloth dipped in rubbing alcohol, then pour a few drops of lemongrass-scented oil on the tip of a paintbrush and spread it over the entire inner surface of the glass.

2 Pour the first layer of powder wax about 1 inch deep.

3 Pour a second layer of wax of another color, making sure the two colors do not mix. Proceed in this way until you've created the layered effect you like.

HINT

Powder wax is peculiar in that only the grains that come into contact with the flame will actually melt. Once the wick has burned, therefore, you can discard it and reuse the intact grains to make another candle.

4 Insert the pointed tip of a skewer along the inner edge of the glass, and "fish" out some color from the first layer. Gently inch the stick around the glass so the first layer of wax next to the glass is slightly mixed with the second, creating a wavelike effect around the circumference of the candle.

5 Insert a waxed wick into the center of the candle, being careful not to disturb the waves you made. A good way to do this is to first insert a skewer through the center to make a hole for the wick.

Africa-Inspired Candle

These opaque candles are layered in warm shades of yellow, orange, and brown and decorated with embossed designs. The patchouli scent, with its slightly intense fragrance, makes this a perfect candle for lighting a nature-inspired living room or favorite reading nook.

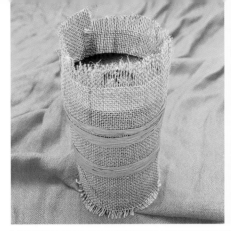

As Gifts

This candle is made for wrapping in natural gift wrap. Cut a piece of rough burlap slightly larger than the size of the candle. Wrap the candle tightly in the burlap, then hold the edges closed while you wrap a couple strands of raffia around the candle.

Another Idea

A unique way to decorate this candle is to write a couple lines of your favorite poem on the side using the liquid wax pen. Personalize the phrase, making a truly heartfelt gift.

To Make the Candles

Materials

- Empty milk carton
- 4 ½ oz opaque wax
- Dark green, brown, orange, and yellow coloring
- White waxed wicks
- Liquid wax pens in white, dark green, and bronze
- Patchouli-scented oil

Equipment

- Double boiler
- Spoon
- Scissors
- Skewer
- Cylindrical mold

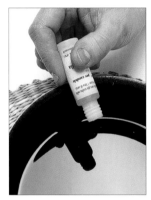

1 Melt approximately 1½ ounces of opaque wax in a double boiler over low heat. Color it with dark green coloring. Continue to stir and add 5 or 6 drops of patchouli-scented oil.

2 Cut the bottom from a milk carton to make a mold about 4 inches high. Pour a layer of green wax about 1½ inches high into the mold. Wrap the end of the wick around a skewer and lay it vertically on the mold's rim. Let the wax cool completely. Make wax for the second layer using 1 ounce of wax colored with brown coloring. Add the second layer, and then another layer of green when the second is solid.

HINT

To avoid mixing the wax colors and to make preparation easier, use two different small pots for the double boiler. After you have made the brown layer, simply reheat the green wax used for the first layer.

3 When the wax has completely hardened, trim the wick and remove the candle from the mold by carefully tearing off the carton.

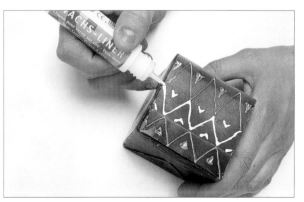

4 Draw symbols and lines on the brown layer using a white liquid wax pen; use a bronze-colored pen on the green layers. Let the candle dry for at least 12 hours. To make the other candle, use a cylindrical mold and alternate wax layers of brown, orange, and yellow. Decorate using dark green and bronze-colored wax pens.

Wooden Inlaid Candle

Adorned with elegant patterns cut from brown wax sheets, these candles appear to be carved from wood. The patterns are attached to a patchouli-scented candle simply by applying light pressure. The warm, musky scent of the patchouli is slowly released in the air, dispersing its calming fragrance.

An Alternative

Use light and dark brown wax sheets to create a wooden star candle. Cover every side of the wax star, alternating between dark and light to create a shadowed effect. For a more intense fragrance, add a few drops of patchouli-scented oil to a cotton ball and swab the surface of the candle and the wax sheets.

How, When, Where

Use these "wooden" inlaid candles to add an elegant touch and calming scent to any room. If you prefer a soft, sweet scent, use sandalwood-scented oil, known for easing tension and stimulating creativity.

To Make the Candle

Materials
- Dark and light brown wax sheets with wood-grain patterns
- Patchouli-scented candle

Equipment
- Scissors
- Hair dryer
- Pen or pencil
- Thin sheet of cardboard

Patterns for the designs (enlarge 100 percent)

HINT

Before heating the wax sheets with a hair dryer, spend some time molding them to the candle with your fingers. Your body heat will cause the wax to lose some of its rigidity, making it malleable enough to attach to the candle.

1 Cut a sheet of dark brown wax that will cover the candle, remove its protective film, and wrap it around the candle. Heat the candle first with a hair dryer to ensure the wax sheet molds to the candle.

2 Place the base of the candle on a dark brown wax sheet, trace the circumference with a pen, and cut out the circle. Pierce a hole through the center.

3 Place the wax disk over the wick, making sure it covers the top of the candle, and heat it with a hair dryer until it softens.

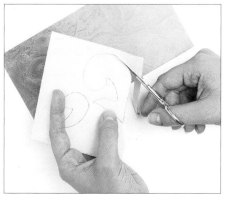

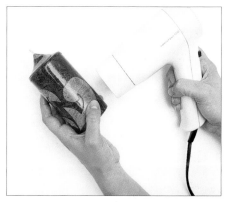

4 Draw a few designs on a piece of thin cardboard, using the patterns. Cut out the designs and trace them on the back of a light brown wax sheet, then cut them out of the wax.

5 Attach the designs to the dark brown candle with your hands. Heat for a few seconds with a hair dryer to mold the pieces together.

Autumn Candle

Burgundy candles, with their deep wine shade, are reminiscent of autumn leaves and brisk evenings spent curled up by the fire. Yellow wax leaves adorning the sides of the candles continue the autumnal theme.

An Alternative

Use wax sheets to create a breakfast mug candle. Cover the inner sides of a clear glass mug with a rectangle of blue marble-patterned wax measured and cut to fit. Heat the wax with a hair dryer to mold it to the walls. Fill the mug with blue powder wax: As they melt, the wax grains will blend with the wax sheet to create a colorful effect.

As Gifts

Create a golden candleholder for these candles. Take a strip of gold-colored cardboard and glue the two ends together to make a circle slightly larger than the base of the candle. Wrap a blue cord around the cardboard, attaching it with hot glue. Glue the candle to the golden candleholder, and wrap the gift in gold-colored netting tied with a deep blue ribbon.

To Make the Candles

Materials

- Rounded candle approximately 4 inches in diameter
- Cubical candle
- Blue wax sheets with a marble design
- Metallic gold liquid wax pen
- Anise-scented oil

Equipment

- Cotton ball
- Pen or pencil
- Scissors

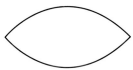

Pattern for rounded candle covering

HINT

To make the wax segments mold to the curves of the candle, gently press them with your hands until they are soft and more malleable. When you have finished covering the candle, hold a hair dryer about 12 inches from the candle and heat the wax segments until they mold together.

1 To make the oval candle, add a few drops of anise-scented oil to a cotton ball and swab it over the wax sheets. Let dry for several minutes.

2 Enlarge the pattern, then trace it on the back of a marbled wax sheet four times.

3 Cut out the four segments with a pair of scissors, being careful not to damage the wax.

4 Hold a wax segment between your hands to heat it, then remove the protective film and place it on the candle. Make sure the tips of the segment are at the wick and the base. Mold it to the surface of the candle by gently smoothing it with your hands. Repeat with the other three segments to cover the candle.

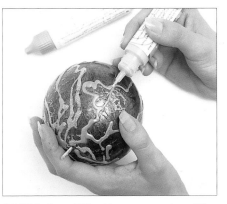

5 With the gold liquid wax pen, paint additional veins of marble. Let the wax dry for at least 2 hours. Make the cubical candles using the same method, measuring and cutting six wax sheets for the sides of each candle.

Flowered Sphere Candle

A stylish spherical candle can easily be embossed using adhesive wax sheets. The colors and designs mimic the traditional style of *azulejos*, Portuguese tin-glazed ceramic tile work. These candles are ideal for decorating a blue and white dinner table, or one that is simply all white.

An Alternative

Even if you think you lack creative skills, you can still make a beautiful candle. Follow the same method used to make the flowered candle, only using this pattern, and you can mimic an intricate ceramic design. Put this candle in your foyer beside two ceramic vases, one white and one blue, for an impressive display.

To Make the Candle

Materials

- Blue spherical candle
- 2 adhesive wax sheets, 1 white and 1 yellow

Equipment

- Pen or pencil
- Small scissors
- Craft knife
- Sheet of paper

1 On a sheet of paper, trace the flower and leaf designs from the pattern. Cut them out with scissors so you can use them as templates.

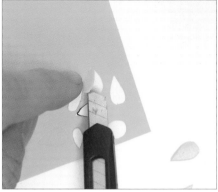

2 Put the paper patterns on the adhesive wax sheets; on the yellow sheet, use the petals, on the white sheet, use the leaves. Cut out approximately fifteen full flowers with leaves, arranging them neatly to conserve space.

HINT

This candle is made with adhesive wax sheets, which are easy to outline but delicate to handle. When using paper patterns, cut out all of the designs from the smallest portion of wax you can so that you can save unused wax for future projects. To store the uncut portions, carefully wrap them in plastic and store in a cool, clean place.

Pattern for the flowers and leaves

3 Carefully position the wax pieces on the spherical candle. Create a five-petaled flower surrounded by small groups of white leaves. Repeat this process until the candle is covered in tiny flowers. Press lightly on the designs so they attach securely to the candle.

143

Lace Candle

White lace doilies dress up these cylindrical sage-colored candles. Both the candle and the wax are scented with sandalwood, which releases a sweet and balmy fragrance to create a soothing and harmonizing atmosphere.

An Alternative

Design cheerful little place-holders for your guests: Make a wax square and a circle of two different colors, pierce through both centers with a needle and insert a waxed wick. Experiment with tone on tone or contrasting colors to create a bright, geometric effect.

How, When, Where

For a children's party, make these colorful candles and add fun citrus scents. For an outside party, use citronella or lavender fragrances, which are both good for repelling insects. To intensify any fragrance, add 2 drops of oil at the base of the wick.

To Make the Candle

Materials

- White wax flakes, 1 oz per candle
- Wax crayons in orange, red, lilac, violet-blue, blue, green apple, and mint green
- Waxed wick
- Square cardboard cartons (1 carton for each layer)
- Lemongrass-scented oil

Equipment

- Double boiler
- Spoon
- Craft knife
- Needle

1 Melt 1 ounce of wax flakes in a double boiler over low heat, add 2 drops of lemongrass-scented oil, and crumble a piece of yellow crayon into the wax. Stir to mix the color and fragrance.

2 Cut the bottom off a cardboard carton to make a mold about 1½ inches high. Pour the melted wax into the mold to create a layer about ½ inch high.

3 When the wax has cooled completely, pierce a hole through the center with a needle.

HINT

To make sure the wick doesn't pull out of the candle, use a wick with a metal base, or fold over the wick at the bottom and affix it to the bottom square with a little melted wax. You can also use modeling clay on the bottom to hold the wick, but you'll need to spread it out so the candle lies flat.

4 Carefully remove the hardened wax square by tearing off the carton.

5 Make other colorful wax squares using the same method and varying the colors. Layer a pile of finished wax squares one on top of the other, alternating colors, until you obtain the desired effect. Insert a waxed wick through the center holes.

Cutout Shape Candle

The sunshine of summer is reflected in these candles made from bright red and orange wax. They're made with two wax layers; the top one is engraved with a flower or star shape. Spicy cinnamon combines with sweet mandarin orange to create an energizing and balancing fragrance.

As Gifts

Use warm red and orange colors to package this gift: Crumple two pieces of colored tissue paper around the candle and tie with a raffia ribbon onto which you've threaded a tag in the same shape as the cutout design. For a fragrant touch, spray a few drops of cinnamon or mandarin-scented oil on the paper.

Scenting the Candle

Mandarin essence has long been used to scent the home and in aromatherapy because of the fruit's many therapeutic properties. A natural antiseptic, mandarin harmonizes and soothes the spirit; it's also used to relieve stress. Spray a little mandarin essence in the house or office to fight fatigue and recapture your energy.

To Make the Candles

Materials
- 5 ½ oz wax per candle
- Waxed wicks
- Square-based cardboard cartons
- Red and orange colorings
- Cinnamon and mandarin-scented oils

Equipment
- Double boiler
- Needle
- Scissors
- Star and flower-shaped cookie cutters
- Tweezers
- Spoon

1 Melt 3 ½ ounces of wax in a double boiler over low heat. Add 5 drops of cinnamon-scented oil and 6 drops of red coloring.

2 Use scissors to cut off the bottom half of a carton. Suspend the wick vertically, supported by a needle or skewer lying across the carton's top rim. Pour a layer of melted wax approximately 1 ½ inches high into the mold.

3 When the wax has partially solidified, untie the wick from the needle and press a small flower-shaped cookie cutter into the center of the wax, about ½ inch deep.

HINT

When you make the orange wax layer, be careful not to pour it inside the cookie cutter. To prevent this, you can cover the top of the cutter with heat-resistant adhesive tape.

4 Melt the remaining wax and add 5 drops of orange coloring and 4 drops of mandarin-scented oil. Pour the wax into the mold, around the flower, filling to the top of the cookie cutter.

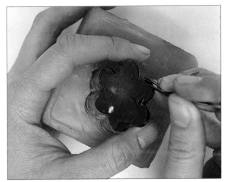

5 When the candle has completely hardened, remove it by gently tearing off the carton. Use tweezers to carefully pull the cookie cutter out of the wax. Repeat the process for the star candle, alternating the colors.

Easter Egg Candle

Partake in a time-honored Easter tradition with a new twist on painted eggs. Liquid wax pens make it easy to design little circles and teardrops on the eggs in classic pastel shades. Rose-scented oil, swabbed on the surface of the eggs, releases a sweet and intense fragrance perfect for welcoming the spring season.